In the Pres

By Therese Hackett Martin

Copyright © 2006 by Therese Martin

All rights reserved; no portion of this book may be published by any medium, except for brief quotations for the purposes of review, without the express permission of the author/publisher.

This book is a work of fiction. While it is loosely based on the author's family history, characters and events have been altered for the purpose of telling a story, and it is not intended to accurately represent any real persons, places, or event, except symbolically. One incident, however, is entirely real; the limousine ride with General MacArthur.

To my mother, Evelyn Rogers Hackett:
Always a heroine, always a lady.
I miss you, Mom.

Chapter One

The syncopated strains of swing music drifted on the warm breeze as Emily Coates walked up the wide steps to the veranda of the Manila Army-Navy Club. Her shoulder-length chestnut bob ruffled softly, a few strands escaping the constraints of bobby pins. It was a beautiful evening, December 7, 1941, and she was 22, footloose and fancy-free. Best of all, she had most of the evening off for the first holiday party of the Christmas season, which in Manila began early in December and lasted until after January 6. Tonight there would be dinner, then dancing, and not a thought of work need cross her mind for at least three hours. She wasn't due in the office until noon, since she had telex duty tonight-- but that was later, and she needn't think about it.

"Emily! You made it! I thought you were going to be stuck in that poky old office all night." Emily turned to see Pat O'Bannion, her best chum and fellow worker.

"I traded with Lily. I have to go back to check the telexes, but that's all."

"I don't know why you ever signed up for that duty. I sure wouldn't. Having to go to the office at unearthly hours three nights a week isn't my idea of a good time."

"But there are only two of us secretaries whose security clearance is high enough for the telex room. Besides, I get to sleep in the next morning," said Emily, laughing. "You know how I hate getting up early. I like my beauty sleep."

"Well, it's still working. I love that dress! You're one of the few girls I know who looks good in beige."

Emily smiled. The dress was more ivory than beige, the local seamstress' latest effort made from lavishly embroidered native fabrics, and it had turned out well. Little cap sleeves, fitted waist, and gored skirt ... all the details that suited her.

"Thanks, Pat. That's a nice outfit, too," she said, admiring her friend's lemon-yellow chiffon dance dress, which flattered her in spite of the fashion dictum that said blondes shouldn't wear yellow. "Is it new?"

"Yes, isn't it a dream? Bought it off the rack, believe it or not." Pat fluttered her white lace fan.

"Really? Where?"

"Hey, just a minute. You girls aren't going to spend the whole evening talking about clothes, are you? There's a party going on!"

Lt. Milton Washburn, known to his friends as "Miltie," a newly commissioned naval medical officer recently posted to Sangley Point, had stepped out onto the veranda. His cheerful grin showed rows of perfect teeth, and his white dress uniform was as impeccable as always. Emily smiled back at him. He was her favorite escort of the moment--handsome, fun loving, attentive.

Washburn smiled at Pat. "Miss O'Bannion, may I introduce the worst tennis player in the Pacific? Ensign Joe Grady, newest addition to the Fleet. Joe, meet Pat O'Bannion, one of the lovely stenographers with the Army Air Corps."

"Pleased to meet you, ma'am," the red-haired young officer said in a pleasant Southern drawl as he took Pat's hand.

"You too, Ensign. We'll have to take you out on the courts and see if Miltie's claim is true. You see, I think I'm the worst tennis player in the Pacific. You'll have to work hard to match my record. I haven't won a single match in the last two years," said Pat.

"Emily, Ensign Joe Grady; Joe, this is Emily Coates, also with the Air Corps, and definitely off-limits," Washburn said, with a meaningful look in his blue eyes.

"Pleased to meet you too, ma'am. I swear, it doesn't seem fair for those flyboys to have the prettiest stenographers in town."

Emily accepted the compliment with a smile, but realized she was mildly annoyed at Miltie for saying she was off-limits. They weren't engaged or anything and the comment seemed unnecessarily possessive. This wasn't even a date! Unlike private functions, the Army-Navy club dances were one of the few occasions where it was respectable for young, single female admin staff to show up dateless. Emily usually preferred it that way. Dining and dancing with other military personnel at these functions didn't imply a commitment, and therefore was less likely to cause gossip than just going out on the town with a gentleman.

"Will you ladies do us the honor of having dinner with us? The buffet looks wonderful," Washburn said, extending his arm to Emily. "Then we can dance the night away and watch the sunrise from the veranda."

"Delighted," said Emily, pushing her annoyance to the back of her mind. After all, it was a party. "Remember, though, I turn into a pumpkin at 0145." At his blank look, she added, "I have telex duty tonight. The car picks me up at quarter till, to get me back to the office by two in the morning."

"That's outrageous. I call it cruel and unusual punishment, taking a lovely lady away from a party. What's so important it can't wait till later?"

"Oh, it's usually routine traffic, but sometimes it gets interesting," Emily said, evasively. The situation these days was anything but routine, but she wasn't about to let the Navy see her concern. Let them ask their own intelligence people--the Air Corps had its secrets, and she wasn't about to let anything slip.

Just last week, in fact, she'd logged in a top-secret coded telex from one of the most respected "deep cover" intelligence operatives in the Pacific. She decoded the message and passed it on to her boss. His comment had been evasive, but she could tell he didn't put much stock in it. She was still worried, though. The telex warned of an imminent attack by the Japanese, and identified the most likely target as Pearl Harbor, the U. S. military base on the island of Oahu in the Hawaiian Islands. This wasn't the first such warning, but coming from this particular operative, Emily thought it deserved more attention than her boss had given it. Nevertheless, it wasn't her job to make those decisions. She was only a secretary, and in her off time, she wanted to enjoy herself, not spend her time worrying about the war. She gave herself a mental shake, widened her smile, and resolved to have a good time this evening.

Emily and Pat preceded the officers into the dining room where linen-draped buffet tables displayed a sumptuous variety of foods. After filling their plates with delicacies from all over the Pacific, the foursome found a table not too far from the dance floor and set out with a will to enjoy the evening.

The food was excellent--grilled seafood, rare roast beef, exotic fruits, vegetables, curries, rice, and exquisite pastries. The conversation, too, was excellent, even if it did ignore the cloud looming in all their minds.

The entire question of whether Japan would move to invade the Philippine Islands in defiance of the United States' mantle of protection was one for serious discussion, not to be talked about when the music was lively, the girls were pretty, and the young men were handsome. Emily was determined to pretend, if just for the evening, that the Empire of Japan didn't exist. Those worries could wait for the morning, when they were all back in khaki uniforms and tailored office suits instead of dress whites and evening gowns.

The band, made up entirely of local musicians, played American hit songs made popular by the best of the big bands. They weren't bad at all, Emily decided as she twirled around the floor to the strains of Glen Miller's "In the Mood." Most of the office staff complained about living in the

Philippines, about the food, the climate, the people. Emily didn't understand them. What could be better than this delightful tropical evening, with marvelous food and dreamy music?

Back at their table during a break in the music, she brought up that question. "Pat," she said, "You've got to admit you can't get anything like this back in the States--unless you're a millionaire, that is."

"You're right. Back home it'd be sandwiches and a record player, on my budget. This is the life, all right--except for the bugs, snakes and lizards. Ugh! I still can't get used to sleeping under a mosquito net."

"It's not so bad."

"Well, Emily, you grew up with it. I didn't. I'll be glad to get home to Minnesota."

"You grew up here?" asked Ensign Grady. "How did that happen? Were your parents missionaries?"

"No, my father came over with General Pershing after the last war, and was appointed to a position with the territorial government. He liked it, and decided to stay. There are lots of Americans who were born here and who have lived here all their lives. It's different, but we like it."

"Wow! I guess I never realized that. I thought all Americans were here with the military."

"It seems that way sometimes, but there are lots of private citizens. Many businesses in Manila are owned and run by Americans, you know."

"No, I didn't know. So you've never lived in the States?"

"Not even for a day. Oh, I'll go there sometime. Maybe after all this has blown over," she said, waving her hand vaguely.

"You mean the war."

"Ensign Grady, we're not at war. We're a neutral country," Pat said, rapping him on the knuckles with her fan.

"Yeah, but for how long? Everyone knows Japan is getting ready to attack. The only question is where."

"Probably Singapore," said Pat. "That's the Brits' problem, not ours."

"Have you looked at a map lately? If I were Tojo, these islands would be looking mighty tempting."

11

"I don't want to think about it," Pat said, tossing her head. "This is a party."

"Just like Scarlett O'Hara, right? Well, ma'am, I don't blame you. It's a scary thought, especially for a pretty girl like you."

Emily watched this exchange with a growing feeling of apprehension. Joe was right. Manila was a ripe plum waiting to fall into the Emperor's hands. She knew, from her work in Intelligence, that Washington agreed and was taking steps to bolster up the defense of the Philippine Islands. In fact, she probably knew more about the proposed deployment of the Pacific Fleet than these Naval officers. In spite of the intelligence operative's concerns about Pearl Harbor, the fact remained that Manila was the most likely first target, and they weren't ready yet for a full-scale attack. In about a week, a substantial portion of the Fleet would be relocating from Pearl Harbor to Manila. If only Japan would wait just a bit longer to launch their attack! Emily didn't believe they were looking for peace, regardless of their peace talks in Washington. They wanted control of the Pacific; that was clear from their public pronouncements as well as the secret transmissions intercepted and decoded by G-2's communications experts. The only question was where they would strike first.

Her brow wrinkled as she remembered a series of recent communiqués between her department and Washington. Although her boss hadn't believed it, he'd passed on the operative's warning and suggested that Pearl Harbor, not Manila, would be the target of a first strike attack. Much to her boss' relief, Washington wasn't buying it. They thought the scraps of information G-2 had unearthed pointed to sabotage, not a full-scale attack. They were taking steps to prevent sabotage, such as an increase in security in otherwise-lax Hawaii. They'd even begun to keep the planes bunched together on the runways to make them easier to guard, and were doing the same with the naval fleet. Still, Emily knew the intelligence agent was pretty sure about his information. What if he was right and Pearl was the target? Might all these precautions make the fleet and its accompanying air cover more vulnerable to attack?

"Penny for your thoughts?"

Startled, Emily looked up into Washburn's smiling blue eyes. She smiled back, determined not to show the real reason for her concern. "Oh, just wondering about some friends of mine at Pearl. They were transferred there a month ago, and I was wondering if they were enjoying a party as nice as ours."

"Who do you know at Pearl? I have some buddies there, too."

The conversation turned to names of old friends and funny stories, and all too soon Emily looked at her watch and realized it was time to go.

"So long, everyone. Time for Cinderella to turn into a secretary," she said, laughing. The officers stood up while she rose from her chair and gathered up her tiny evening purse. Waving goodbye, she glided swiftly out of the room as the band struck up a rather odd-sounding rendition of the Andrews Sisters' hit song, "Bei Mir Bist Du Schoen." Somehow, she thought with a chuckle, the German words just didn't sound the same with a Filipino accent. She got her wrap from the coat checkroom and hurried down the wide steps to her waiting car. The driver held the door open for her; she sat carefully on the seat, smoothing her skirt as the driver closed the passenger door.

"Good evening, ma'am," the driver said as the car moved smoothly on to the nearly deserted boulevard. "How was the party?"

"Very nice, thank you, private," Emily said with a polite smile. She stifled a yawn. Regardless of what she'd said to Pat, she had to admit to herself that this late telex duty was a real chore. Well, she'd be home soon enough. It wouldn't take long to get to the telex room, pull the telexes off the printer, and lock them up in the safe in her office. Then she'd be done for the day.

"Hey, is something going on back at the office? I noticed lots of lights on when I checked the car out of the motor pool."

"I don't know of anything. I'm sure I'll find out when I get there--if there's anything I need to know, that is."

The mild rebuke silenced the driver. Soon, the car pulled up to the front entrance of the Army Air Corps' administration office, a block like, two-story building surrounded by half-round Quonset huts. Emily hurried into the building, telling the driver to wait for her.

He'd been right; there was a surprising amount of activity for this hour of the night--actually, morning. Emily passed several lighted doorways as she walked down the long hall to the telex room. Mostly upper brass, she realized, recalling belatedly that she hadn't seen many high-ranking officers at the party. Something really must be going on.

Her boss, Commander Jameson, stepped out of his office. "Oh, good, you're here, Emily. Bring the telexes to me instead of to your office, will you?"

"Yes, sir," she said, digging the key out of her purse.

The telex room, of course, was locked. She unlocked the door and went in. The long roll of telex paper piling up on the floor was evidence of an unusual amount of telex activity. With a large pair of scissors, she cut the strip from the machine an inch after the last message and began cutting the messages apart, skimming them as she snipped. The first couple of messages were routine, but then...

Emily dropped the scissors on the floor. Grabbing the rest of the telex paper in a tangled bunch, she ran down the hall to Jameson's office, pushed through the half-opened door and stopped, breathless.

"What is it, Emily?" Jameson asked, stepping around his desk.

Wordlessly, she handed him the long, tangled strip of paper, pointing to the message that caught her eye.

He gasped, swore under his breath, and picked up the phone. Dimly, as if in a dream, Emily heard him speaking to the operator.

"Mary, get me the general on the line. Quick. Ring his quarters."

Emily leaned against the wall for support, hoping she wouldn't disgrace herself by fainting. Moments later, she heard Jameson again.

"Bill, it's bad. Pearl's been hit."

Chapter Two

The first light of dawn peeked over the horizon as Emily reached home. Her hands shook as she unlocked the door and crept into the silent house. She knew she needed sleep, but doubted she'd be able to rest. Her mind was in turmoil, and her eyes were red-rimmed from weeping.

The news, as it unfolded, was horrific. Pearl Harbor had been attacked from the air. Most of the fleet was destroyed; the death toll was well over a thousand and still rising. All the precautions against sabotage had left the ships and planes vulnerable to enemy attack from the air. Sailors, airmen, nurses, doctors-- military personnel of all kinds were lying dead in makeshift morgues. Even more were wounded, suffering in agony because of the lack of medical help; there just wasn't enough medicine or healthy, surviving personnel to go around. She feared some of her friends were among the dead and wounded, but it would be days, or even weeks, before she knew for sure.

Perhaps worst of all, the United States was now at war with Japan, and because of the Axis agreements, Germany would soon be declaring war on the United States as well. Her country--the shining land she'd never even seen--was in the middle of a two-front world war, and the future looked terrifying.

"Emily? What happened? You're so late." It was her mother's gentle voice, and Emily turned to see her mother, still in her light gray cotton dressing gown and black satin slippers, her graying hair escaping the thick braid that hung down in front of her left shoulder, the familiar face lined with worry.

"Oh, Mama!" Emily's voice broke, and she rushed to embrace her mother. Unable to contain her feelings, she gave way to fierce sobbing, her shoulders shaking with anguish.

"Why, what's the matter?" Her mother patted Emily on the back as if she were a baby. "What on earth happened? Were you in an accident? I warned you about those jitney drivers. You should always ask for a driver from the motor pool, Emily. It's much safer."

"No, Mama," Emily said between sobs, "It wasn't an accident. It's war, Mama. War."

"War? What are you talking about? I don't know about any war. Your father said there wouldn't be any war, and he's always right. Here, blow your nose, stand up straight, take a deep breath, and tell me what's wrong." Margarete Coates had very little tolerance for emotional displays, and Emily knew it didn't mean her mother didn't care about her. It was just the way she was. No matter what, she remained calm. Relatives even said that, when Margarete was seventeen and her father was beheaded by assassins right in front of her in their dining room, she even fainted in a ladylike way, with no outcry; she'd just slipped silently under the dining table and lay, unconscious, with her clothing neatly arranged. That probably saved her life. The assassins didn't know she was there. Family rumor said that when she regained consciousness, her first concern was for her mother; assured that she was uninjured, she then called for servants to clean up the blood on the floor, and calmly went to comfort her mother.

"Mama," Emily said, exasperated but obeying her. She took the handkerchief, wiped her eyes, blew her nose, stood up straight, and took a deep breath.

"Papa is a Quaker, Mama. He doesn't believe in war. Sometimes I think he's not even sure war exists. He doesn't want to think about it. You know how he is. He always thinks the best of everyone. You've complained about that often enough."

"I don't know what you're talking about. I never complain about your father. That wouldn't be right. I might offer my opinion, but I never complain."

"Of course, Mama. I used the wrong word. I should have said you've expressed yourself on that subject. Forgive me."

"You need to expand your vocabulary. Sometimes I think working with all those soldiers isn't quite ladylike. It seems to have coarsened your speech."

"I'm sure you're right, Mama. But this has nothing to do with being ladylike. It really is war."

"Then we need to discuss this. Let's go into the kitchen and talk. I'll make some tea. The maids won't be up for at least another hour, so we'll have privacy. You can tell me all about it, and we can figure out what to do to keep the children safe."

The children, Annabelle and Charlotte, were nine and fourteen. Another sister, Jeannette--"Jeannie" for short--was eighteen. Jeannie fell midway between "child" and "young lady" in their mother's estimation, and Emily wasn't sure that, in this crisis, her mother wasn't mentally categorizing her second daughter with the little ones. Jeannie had always seemed younger; she was blonde, frivolous, and even less capable of taking care of herself than Charlotte, who loved reading adventure stories, liked to be called "Charlie," and claimed she wanted to be a pilot when she grew up. Amelia Earhart was Charlie's heroine, as were Queen Elizabeth I of England and the ancient Briton woman warrior-chief, Boadicea.

As if reading her daughter's thoughts, Margarete said, "You know Charlie will want to enlist in the WAVES if this is really a war." Her calm, capable hands showed no sign of trembling as she packed tea in the tea strainer and turned up the heat under the kettle. It began to whistle almost at once; Emily realized Mama must have been waiting up for her, and had probably already had at least one cup of tea this morning. She watched as Margarete picked up the plain stoneware mug she'd been using, put it in the sink, and set out her favorite tea set, the one she always used in a crisis; it was English china from Hong Kong, a wedding gift from one of the sultans of the southern Philippine islands. Deep pink roses and green vines encircled the graceful lines of the teapot, cups and saucers, just as they'd done for more than twenty years. Emily sighed as she sat at the scrubbed wooden table. No matter what was happening in the world, some things didn't change, and Mama and her tea set were among the unchangeable.

"She can't, Mama. She's only fourteen, and she looks about twelve. Even if she tried lying about her age, no one would believe her. Besides, everyone at the base knows her--she's always hanging around asking questions."

"That's true." Margarete handed Emily a cup of tea. "Here you are, dear. Now, tell me all about it."

Emily took the cup gratefully, her hands curling around the thin, hand-painted china. With nerves soothed by her mother's calming presence, Emily was able to talk coherently about what had happened that morning.

Beginning with the telex that brought the news about the attack on Pearl Harbor, she told her mother about the long distance phone calls, telexes and radio messages that flew across the Pacific and on to Washington and back again. She told her about the attacks on the other three bases on Oahu; the mounting death toll; and, finally, the report of President Roosevelt's call to Congress for a declaration of war, calling December 7 "a day that will live in infamy."

"It really is war, then, Emily."

"Yes, Mama. It really is."

"We have to contact your father immediately."

"Mama, we can't. The phone lines are taken up with war traffic, and I doubt we could even get a telegram through right now. I'm sure he'll try to get to Manila as quickly as he can. We'll just have to wait."

"If the Japanese land here, we'll be cut off from everything. How will he get through? He's not a fighting man." Margarete said the words as if "fighting man" was an insult--and, to her, it was.

"He'll get through somehow, I'm sure. Besides, maybe they won't land. Maybe we'll be able to fight them off. I just wish there was something we could do to help."

Her mother looked at her in disapproval. "Of course there's something we can do. There always is. I'm surprised at you." At Emily's questioning look, she added, "We can pray. We can always pray." She pushed back her chair and then tucked it back neatly under the table. "That's what I'm going to do, as soon as I wake Jeannie and Charlie and get the yayas started on waking Annabelle and getting her dressed. The cook will be here any moment. I'll leave you to tell her what's happened. After breakfast, we'll have a family council and make some decisions."

A family council without Papa? Unheard of! Numbly, Emily nodded as her mother left the room, her back ramrod-straight, her head held high. If anyone's prayers could stop a

25

war, Margarete's surely could. Emily finished her tea, and then went upstairs to have a quick shower and change into something more suitable for a war council than a party dress.

...

"But, Mama, I don't understand. Why do we have to do all that sewing? Why can't the maids do it?" Jeannie's normally pleasant voice whined. She hated sewing.

"Because we don't want them to know what we're doing," Margarete explained patiently, with an air of long-suffering. "If they don't know, they can't tell, and they won't have to lie. I will not ask my servants to lie."

Jeannie pouted. "But that's such a lot of work, and I always prick my fingers. This stupid war is ridiculous. I had so many plans and parties to go to, and now they'll probably all be cancelled, and on top of that, I have to sew my fingers to the bone just so the maids won't have to lie. Who cares if they lie, anyway? They won't be sinning, because they're only obeying your orders, and you won't be sinning because you aren't the one doing the lying."

"Jeannie, you are being disrespectful. You will do as I say, and I'll hear no more about it. Do you understand?"

"But, Mama, this is wartime. Aren't we allowed to lie in wartime?" Charlie was fascinated with the idea of war. The news hadn't saddened her, as it had Emily and their mother, or frightened her, as it had little Annabelle. Emily recognized the signs. She was exhilarated, her eyes sparkling with excitement. She'd already suggested she should go on foot to the plantation to warn their father, and was crushed when her mother refused in no uncertain terms.

"No, Charlotte. We are not allowed to lie in wartime. One evil does not cancel out another. We are not at war with anyone. This family does not make war. I hope that's quite clear."

"Yes, Mama," said Charlie, unconvinced.

"What do I have to do, Mama?" asked Annabelle.

"Pack a small bag with two changes of underwear, two pairs of socks, an extra pair of shoes, and an old dress. Your blue cotton check would be a good choice. Keep the bag where you can find it right away and if we go out take it with you. Now, I want you to go and read quietly in your room for a little while."

"But what about sewing? You said we had to do a lot of sewing. I want to help."

"No, child, I don't want you to be involved in this part of our plans. You go upstairs now."

"Yes, Mama." Reluctantly, the nine-year-old climbed off her mother's lap and left the study, closing the door behind her.

"Now, girls, I'll explain about the sewing."

"I think I can guess, Mama," said Emily. "Money?"

Margarete smiled and nodded. "That's right. We'll sew paper money into our clothes. I want them spread out so there are no bulges visible. Pick two or three dresses or suits. Make sure they're lined. I don't want to try this with thin cotton or gauze. We'll get old bills so they won't crackle as much. I also want you to pick out two pairs of shoes. They should be a little bit big. Maybe we can buy some shoes in a size too large. That might be best. We'll make new linings out of scrap leather and hide money under the lining. We can put small jewelry items in the toes, if the shoes are big enough."

"You've thought this through, haven't you, Mama?"

"Of course. When I was growing up, there was always a danger of native uprisings. Our skirts were longer and fuller in those days, and I always had money and jewelry sewn in my skirts, just in case we had to leave in a hurry. Ever since we started hearing rumors of war, I've been thinking about this. No matter where we go, we'll need money to buy food and shelter. We can't count on finding charity if the country is occupied by enemy forces. It would be too dangerous for people to help us."

Emily shook her head in amazement. Her calm, quiet mother had been through some incredible experiences in her life, and somehow managed to maintain a serene facade, as if no ripple stronger than a spoiled tea party had ever marred the surface of her existence. Emily was convinced her mother would face the Last Judgment with every hair in place, her gentle hands clasped in front of her, clad in white cotton gloves. The trump would resound, the Lord would descend, and Mama would take it all in stride.

"Oh, Mama, I have a wonderful idea!" Jeannie's pout had disappeared, and she almost bounced up and down in her chair like a child.

Margarete turned her gentle smile on her daughter. "Yes?"

"Why don't we roll up bills and put them in our rats? I'll be glad to do mine and Emily's as well."

Emily grinned. That wasn't a bad idea at all--the "rats" she and Jeannie wore in their hair to give their hairstyles the raised pompadour look were actually rolls made of netting, and some tightly rolled bills would fit in them nicely. Trust Jeannie to figure out a way to get out of sewing!

"We can wear larger rats, too, and fit even more money into them. What do you think, Mama?" Emily asked.

"It's a good idea. You know I don't like these extreme hairstyles, but in this crisis, I'll allow it. I might even wear a small one myself and I think I'll go back to wearing the older fashions, with longer skirts. There, Charlotte, you see I'm making a wartime effort," Margarete said, with a smile.

"Mama, can I start wearing cowboy boots? We could hide lots of money in those."

Her mother frowned. "They aren't very ladylike, Charlotte." She thought for a moment, and then nodded. "I suppose that would be acceptable, but I won't have you wearing trousers. You may wear the boots with skirts."

"Yes, Mama," said Charlie, delighted with this small concession. She loved wearing her cowboy boots.

"Well, girls, let's get started. I'll go to the bank and see how much money I can take out. I'll also buy some seeds for planting. We may as well be prepared for any eventuality."

Margarete sailed out of the room, almost as if she were already wearing the longer skirts Emily suspected she was longing to put on. Charlie went to find her boots and the most Western-looking dresses she owned, and Jeannie sauntered off in search of large rats.

Emily sighed deeply, rubbed her temples, and went to her own room to get ready for a meeting of the American Coordinating Committee. Because of her high security position, she wasn't a voting member on the committee, but attended the meetings whenever she could to keep informed. The Committee had requested evacuation of all non-essential American civilian personnel some months earlier, but the request had been denied by the military command. This meeting would probably be unpleasant, full of recriminations. Nevertheless, she knew her superiors would expect her to attend--not precisely as a spy, but certainly to keep them "in the know" regarding civilian sentiment. Maybe she'd better take an aspirin or two before going. It was going to be a long evening.

Chapter Three

The days following the news about Pearl Harbor hung heavy on the islands, with a muggy weight that presaged a storm. The weather mirrored everyone's temperament. The holiday mood was gone, and in its place was a grim endurance. All too soon, the attack on Manila would come.

Emily breathed deeply as she left the office late one night. She was exhausted. The news from the war front was not good. The Japanese were closing in. Bombing raids near the city were a daily fact of life, with air-raid sirens sending out their banshee wails with terrifying regularity. She was working long hours, interrupted by quick runs to the makeshift bomb shelters whenever the bombers got too close. Tonight had been quiet--so far--and she was looking forward to getting home and falling into bed for a few hours' sleep before starting all over again in the early morning. She'd been excused from the family sewing chores--her mother and sisters had it well under control, and she was sorely needed on the job.

Just as she prepared to hail a taxi, the air raid siren sounded. People poured out of the building as motor pool vehicles drew up in front, filled up with as many people as they could hold, and drove off to the shelters. Emily stood and watched dully; she was too tired to care.

"Emily! Come on! What are you waiting for?" Emily heard someone shout. She looked, and in a black motor pool car just pulling up to the curb she saw Pat hanging halfway out the front passenger window, motioning her to hurry. She squeezed in next to her friend, and only after they left with a screech of tires did she recognize the identity of the officer in the back seat.

"General MacArthur! Good evening, sir," she said, trying not to stammer.

"Good evening, ladies. Need a lift somewhere?"

Emily and Pat giggled nervously. "Yes, sir, thank you," said Emily. "Can you manage a quick trip to San Francisco?"

The General chuckled. "Uh... 'Fraid not, ladies. Will the shelter do?"

"Yes, sir. It will do quite well."

"Well, driver, we have our orders. Let's take the ladies to the shelter."

Just then the all clear sounded. With ill-disguised relief, Emily said, "I guess it was a false alarm. You can let us off here, General. We can share a cab home. We don't live far from each other."

"Not on your life. We're taking you both to your homes. Where do you live?"

"Oh, but General, we couldn't ask you to take us home. We live in the other direction, in Pasay. That's way out of your way."

"Yes, General. We'll be perfectly safe if there isn't a bombing raid," added Pat.

"Girls, you heard me. I'm taking you safely home. This is no town for young ladies to be wandering around in, bombs or no bombs. Now, give the driver your addresses. That's an order."

Meekly, they acquiesced. One just didn't argue with the General of the Army.

A few blocks from their destination, MacArthur drew out his pipe and pulled a box of matches out of his pocket.

The driver, looking in the rear-view mirror, saw what he was doing.

"Umm ... sir, you can't do that," said the young private, a nervous quiver in his voice. "Blackout. No matches."

Emily expected the General to snap angrily at the driver. To her surprise, he nodded, put the pipe and matches away, and apologized. She realized that even CINCPAC--the Commander in Chief of the Armed Forces in the Pacific--was under orders in wartime, and no personal habit was more important than wartime security measures.

"Mama, I was afraid he was going to get angry with the driver," she told her mother later over a cup of tea. "After all, he's General MacArthur! But he didn't."

"Of course not," her mother answered. "He's a man of character. If he weren't, he wouldn't be trustworthy enough to be in his position. Not all our officers are like the young ones you meet at the dances. Some of them are gentlemen, my dear, and that will always be the most important consideration."

During the night, the air raid sirens blared again, and Emily and her family hurried into the root cellar, which they were using as a bomb shelter. In the morning, they learned that Nichols Field, near the Manila suburbs, had suffered damage during the night's bombing. Each new day brought news of injury to the civilian as well as to the military population. Emily and her family worked, sewed, and prayed. Finally, two letters came from Peter Coates--one for Margarete, of course, and one for Emily.

"A letter from Papa for me! What can he want?"

"Well, my dear, you might open it and see."

With fumbling hands, Emily opened the letter.

"Mama, he says he's turning the house and grounds over to the Sison family."

"Yes, I have that in my letter as well. He thinks the property might escape damage if the Japanese believe it belongs to Filipinos rather than Americans."

"So he thinks they'll reach the plantation, then."

Margarete sighed. "Emily, they are almost certainly there by now. This letter was sent days ago."

"Do you think he's been captured?"

"It's possible. All we can do is pray."

Emily fumed inwardly about her mother's perpetual calm. Would nothing ever shake her? Even the prospect of a Japanese invasion hadn't ruffled a hair! She returned to her letter. As she read, she began to feel a premonition of disaster.

"Emily, my dear," her father had written, "Whatever happens to me, you must take care of your mother and your sisters. You are the oldest. I want you to take this as a sacred charge. They are your responsibility. Your mother is a wise woman, but she has suffered so many tragedies and shocks in her life, I don't want her to shoulder the burden alone if I don't return to you. I know I can trust you to accept this responsibility."

Emily shuddered. Was her father suggesting he might die in the war? Unthinkable! Parents should be indestructible.

Logically, she knew it was a foolish thought, but she couldn't help it. She hurriedly put the letter away, and tried not to think about it, but over the next days, his words kept coming back to her in a recurring refrain. "Accept this responsibility-- accept this responsibility---"

Well before Christmas, the Japanese began their invasion of the Philippines and made their way slowly to the capital. Manila waited anxiously for the enemy to come. Hoping to minimize civilian casualties, General MacArthur declared Manila an "open city" and moved his troops out of Manila to Corregidor and the Bataan Peninsula. On December 27, bombs fell directly on Manila. Fires burned across the city, making blackout precautions useless. Fires from exploding oil dumps lighted up the skies; oil ran along the banks of the river, outlining the water in flame. They were lit up by flaming beacons for any passing aircraft to see and target. Residents of Manila--Filipino and expatriate--waited for the inevitable. They didn't have long to wait. On January 2, the first Japanese troops entered the city.

Emily woke up on the morning of January 5 to unusual silence. No bombs, no sound of gunfire in the neighborhood. She dressed quickly in the specially prepared clothing and went down to the kitchen. Her mother was waiting, having a cup of coffee.

"Good morning, Mama. Are you alone? Where are the maids? Out shopping?"

"No, Emily. They're gone. They're afraid to stay in an American house. I sent them home to their families. We'll be fine."

"Of course we will, Mama. We've had to cope without servants before. I remember that really bad year we had, when I was twelve. We had to send the household staff away because we couldn't even afford to feed them. We could barely feed ourselves after the crops failed, remember? Christmas dinner that year was a chicken."

"Sally. The chicken's name was Sally. She was one of my best layers. I hated to cook her, but she was the oldest and it was just a matter of time before she stopped producing eggs. I didn't want you children to go without any Christmas dinner. Poor Sally."

"Mama, I know it was hard to give up one of your hens. Those were hard times. My Christmas present that year was Papa's old jackknife. It was awful, but we survived. Are the girls up yet?"

"Jeannie has had breakfast. She's working on making rats out of money. She seems to be enjoying the work, so I don't want to discourage her. The little ones are still asleep."

"Good. They need their rest. They had nightmares all night. Annabelle woke up crying twice. Is there any news?"

"Nothing good. Those people are using Santo Tomas campus as a prison camp. They took three hundred people there yesterday." Margarete refused to dignify their enemies by any name other than "those people."

"The university? Why?"

"I suppose because it's large, there are walls and gates, and it has dormitories and kitchen facilities. It would make a suitable prison camp for civilians."

"Civilians? Can they do that?"

"Evidently. They have already done it, dear. There is no use resisting. They have guns. What can we do? They say they will put all enemy aliens in concentration camps. Imagine. We are classified as enemy aliens."

"Any word from Papa?"

"No. Nothing since the letters we got last month. I'm very concerned about him. I know if it were at all possible, he would be here. If he hasn't been captured ... I hope he hasn't tried to walk to Manila through the fighting."

"Mama, he's too sensible. He's probably staying in the village, keeping out of trouble. You'll see. He'll get a message to us somehow."

Her mother sighed. "We'd better be prepared for anything. Let's pack some bags. They might let us bring luggage with us."

"What if they don't? I've heard that some people who were arrested weren't allowed to bring anything with them."

"We'll be prepared either way. At least it's something to do."

Together, they went to the storage building behind the house and brought in four suitcases and four large handbags. They had no hope of bringing any more. Then, Emily and her mother made lists of the things they should bring, making sure they had pockets sewn in all their skirts. Some of them were made with double layers of fabric; Margarete had been sewing for days, and had constructed double dresses that could be easily taken apart. These were the dresses they decided to wear, so they would be ready with at least two dresses each if they weren't allowed to take suitcases. They sewed pockets into the skirts and petticoats, wearing multiple layers of petticoats as well. It was warm, but the risk justified the minor discomfort. It would be terrible to be imprisoned for days, perhaps even weeks, with only one thin dress.

Margarete made sure she had needles sewn in her dress, and Emily removed the thread from several spools, winding it around bits of cardboard so it would be easier to hide in their clothing. The money, of course, was in their shoes and hair rats, and jewelry was sewn into their skirts and hidden under a false bottom in their suitcases. They kept a good amount of cash in their purses, easy for anyone to see, hoping that if their captors found enough money to keep them happy they wouldn't look any further. Then, the actual packing began.

Chapter Four

Getting the contents of their bags together proved to be more difficult than Emily had expected. What to bring? How to arrange it? Each bag had to contain something for each of them, on the chance that they'd only be able to take one bag for the whole family. Each of the four bags contained the same thing. A change of underwear and a cotton dress for each of them; nightwear; toothbrushes; extra footwear and stockings; that was about all. Emily added Bermuda shorts and shirts for the younger girls, but knew Margarete would disapprove of shorts for her and Jeannie. This way, each of them had three dresses-the one packed and the two they wore-and two pairs of shoes, plus native sandals to use as slippers. Margarete insisted on including a bottle of vitamins and a basic first-aid kit in each bag. A former nurse, she was always worrying about the family's health. Along with packing, breakfast and lunch had to be prepared. There was no sense in missing any meals, especially since once arrested they might miss a good many of them. Margarete made sure the house was spotless--she did not want "those people" to think Americans didn't know how to clean without servants.

In the middle of the afternoon, a knock on the door echoed through the house. Emily went to answer it. A Japanese officer stood there, with two armed soldiers standing at attention behind him.

"Yes?" Emily questioned. "Can I help you?"

"You come with us." He spoke in a clipped tone, with a heavy accent, as if unfamiliar with the language. "All who are in this house must come with us. You will bring clothing for two days. Hurry and make haste. You must be ready in five minutes," he said, reading from a slip of paper in his hand.

"Where are we going?"

"You come with us," he repeated, stone-faced. The soldiers behind him looked as if they were all too ready to use their weapons. "This by order of the Imperial Army of Japan. All who are in this house must come with us."

"Yes, I understand. We will come with you. Please tell me where we are going. My mother is old and she will be afraid," said Emily, remembering that the Japanese were respectful of the elderly.

The man's face softened. "Tell your mother we go to University San Tomas. You will not be harmed. You are all ladies in this house. We have searched records. Ladies are in danger in the city. Many soldiers. You understand? You will be safe in University." He paused, as if searching for words. "I have mother also. I do not want my mother to be in danger. You want same. You come with us. Safer."

"Thank you. I will tell my mother. We will come with you," Emily repeated, and closed the door, leaving it a little bit ajar.

They followed their pre-arranged plan. Emily, Jeannie and Margarete remained downstairs while the younger girls ran up to use the bathroom. Jeannie grabbed the money-stuffed rats and added them to their hairdos. Then they took turns using the bathroom, and within the prescribed five minutes were ready to go, both bags in hand. They also took their purses, which contained only a small amount of money and basic cosmetics. Jewelry and money were distributed throughout their clothing, sewn carefully into the linings and pockets, and also beneath the lining of the four suitcases, which to Emily's delight they were allowed to bring; one bag per person, the officer said.

Their precautions were wise. The soldiers checked their purses and took the money "for safety," and gave the contents of the bags a cursory glance, but didn't check the clothing or their hair. Margarete had thought that having no money on them would stir up suspicion, and she was right. The soldiers were content with what they confiscated from the purses- about a week's pay, a believable sum for them to have on hand. Emily sighed in relief; she and her family had the better part of a year's income on their persons, and even at black market prices they would be able to buy food for a while and pay some necessary bribes. They were careful to be polite to the soldiers; even Charlie acted quiet and demure. The Coates family followed the soldiers out the door, locking it carefully behind them, knowing they might never return.

The two-day stay promised by the officer turned into three, then a week, then two weeks, then a month. March arrived, and Emily and her family were still in Santo Tomas--now renamed Santo Tomas Internment Camp.

With typical Yankee organization and ingenuity, the nearly 4,000 internees had organized themselves into a community. They had elected officials, set up kitchens, and arranged for provisions to be brought in. The Executive Committee, which is the name they gave to the camp government, was mostly made up of people with high-level management experience in international corporations. They certainly had the expertise needed for the job. Whenever possible, they tried to solve their own problems and present the Japanese officials with a workable solution. In most cases, they were pleased to have the problems taken care of and agreed to the internees' plans.

Internees were assigned jobs. Emily's job was working as a secretary for the Executive Committee. She did general typing and mimeographing, and soon was helping to create educational materials for the new school the internees started up for the children. Her sister Jeannie helped out in the first aid office, since she had a little bit of first aid training. Margarete planned to work as a teacher when the school was set up. Even Charlotte had a job. She helped build tables and other needed items for the camp.

The conditions in the university dormitories were crowded and unsanitary. The Santo Tomas campus was about sixty-five acres of well-landscaped lawns, with buildings in the Spanish Colonial style, mainly of gray concrete, surrounded by high stone walls. The front gates were wrought iron, as were the bars on the windows. The prisoners were housed in the dormitories in the Main Building, but there were not enough beds for all of them. Most were sleeping on the floor in hallways and classrooms. Some of the Coates family's money stash had gone to buy twenty straw mats, and for the first few weeks they used these as beds, piled four high, stacking them against a wall in the upstairs hallway during the day.

They also spent some of their precious resources for soap and disinfectant, which was nearly as important as food to Margarete. The food provided by their captors was poor quality, mostly starch like rice, yams and occasional biscuits or bread. Margarete bought seeds and planted high-protein crops, soy and lima beans, to supplement the diet. Emily protested; surely they wouldn't be there long enough for the crops to be ready for harvest! Margarete didn't listen, but planted them anyway.

"It's better to be prepared, dear. We may be here a long time."

Emily fumed, but realized her mother was right. She just hated to admit it. She wanted to be out of this place. Toilet facilities were inadequate; Margarete, with her ladylike fastidiousness, found this a trial, but endured it stoically. Often they had to creep outside before dawn to use the one available faucet for washing, since the overcrowding in the dormitory bathrooms left drains plugged and sinks overflowing. The stench was horrendous. Even in the years of financial difficulty, Emily had never known filth like this. They had always had decent housing and scrupulously clean living conditions. When her mother wasn't around, Emily went off by herself and gave way to tears. It wasn't fair. What had they done to deserve this? She started to give up, started to be less careful with her own appearance. After all, what did it matter?

One morning, she woke up and realized her head was itching. Lice! She had lice all through her head, and bedbug bites on her legs. It was still dark, just before dawn. She hurried out of the building to the faucet. Blessedly, there was no one else there. She scrubbed herself with a bit of soap, rinsed her hair several times, and dressed in the cleanest dress she had.

As soon as the sun came up, she went to the health committee and asked for a suggestion for a de-lousing remedy. They did the best they could, but informed her that nearly everyone was struggling with bugs of one kind or another. In fact, even the food was infested with bugs. The older women in camp were assigned to the de-bugging committee, which was a fancy name for the workers who picked bugs out of the flour. Emily remembered her mother had just started on a new position, and she realized that was what Margarete was doing-picking bugs. What a comedown for a woman with two college degrees! Still, Emily realized the teaching position didn't take up the whole day, and her mother had always been happier being busy.

Finally, in late February, internees got permission from the commandant to build shelters, called shanties, on the grounds. Friends in Manila sent building materials, which were hoisted over the eight-foot-high walls.

"Mama!" Charlotte said gleefully as she ran into the dormitory. "They said I can help build shanties! I'm the only girl on the crew. Isn't that wonderful?"

"Charming, dear. Something to add to your list of ladylike accomplishments." The sarcasm was lost on Charlotte, who was proud of being allowed to work on the building crew. The shanties sprang up all over the campus, separated by narrow lanes. Those with more money were able to buy complete prefabricated nipa huts, the traditional homes in Filipino villages. They were quite elaborate, raised up on stilts to keep them out of the floodwaters during monsoons. With windows in each, wall, the cross-ventilation kept them cool. Others built huts on site with lumber brought in over the wall; sometimes the shanties were merely tents made from fabric over a rough wood framework. Still, no matter how rough, they were an improvement on the dormitories.

Half their straw mats, plus some additional lumber, provided the materials the Coates family needed for their new shelter, and by the middle of March Margarete and the two younger girls moved into a shanty built of straw mats nailed to a wood frame. The mats were tightly woven and would provide protection from rain, although during the monsoon season they would cover the mats with waterproof canvas. It was tiny, so after only a few days of crowding together in the shanty Emily and Jeannie volunteered to return to the dormitory.

There was another reason the two older sisters chose to live in the main building, but it wasn't a reason they could share with their mother. They needed to be in the dormitory because the Japanese guards were watching the shanties carefully. In the noise and confusion of the main building, some of their activities might escape notice.

Emily's work for the Army Air Corps before the war was more than just cutting up telexes. She had worked with the intelligence department on many occasions, and some of the wives of those operatives-and even the men themselves, those who were civilians rather than military personnel-were in the camp, under various guises. They quickly formed themselves into a clandestine intelligence unit. The intelligence community in Manila was a closely-knit group, and they knew her skills. Before too long, she was approached by the "in-charge" of the unit, a cheerful, redheaded woman named Christine, who appeared to be a Navy nurse. In fact, although she did have some nursing skills, she was a highly rated field agent.

"Emily, you got a minute?" asked Christine, as they took their tin plates filled with rice and yams from the food serving line.

"Sure thing. What's up?"

"Let's go for a walk. Not too close to the wall, but far enough out so we won't be overheard."

Puzzled, Emily walked along, pretending to reply to Christine's inane remarks about organizing a club to put on birthday celebrations. She knew enough about Christine's real work to go along with the act. Finally, when they were out of earshot, the field agent dropped the pretense.

"Kid, you did some good work in the office. You up for some more of the same?"

"Anything. Who do I have to kill?" Emily asked, flippantly.

Christine laughed. "I don't think it'll come to that. Just make sure you don't get yourself killed, that's all I ask."

"What's the angle? If it's dangerous, it's probably going to really bug our little friends, and I'm game for that. You'd better believe it."

"Atta girl. I knew you had guts. There's this little matter of a radio. See, one thing we have to have is communications. That's the one thing our little friends don't want us to have. We have a radio transceiver.

Obviously, it's too dangerous to leave lying around. Could get someone into a lot of trouble. Matter of fact, it could get someone killed. We need to keep the parts in as many locations as possible, and no one needs to know where the other parts are. When we're going to meet to get a message, we'll let everyone know. From what I hear, you're good at hiding things and keeping your mouth shut. Did I hear right?"

"You heard right," Emily said, trying not to sound frightened. It was one thing to work in the safety of a U. S. government office with the "spooks," as they called the intelligence folks, and quite another to become one herself, right under the noses of the enemy. Nevertheless, she knew she had to do it. It was her duty.

Christine smiled, then handed her a small object wrapped in fabric. From the feel of it, Emily realized it was a radio tube. She nodded and hid the little parcel down the front of her dress. They walked back to the main building together, chattering away about birthday parties. As they reached the front steps, Christine paused.

"You realize you'll have to move back into the dorm?"

"Sure thing. Can't put Mama and the little ones at risk. Besides..."

"Yep. More places to hide things in the dorm. You're quick. That's good. Keeps you healthy. Well, I'll see you around," she said, raising her voice. "I'll let you know when we need to plan a party."

"Sure thing, Chris. See you later." Emily walked off, heading for the family's shanty to tell her mother she was moving back to the dorm. From the smile on her face, she was sure no one could tell she was shaking inside. She had just gotten involved in a clandestine activity that was likely to get her shot.

Chapter Five

Much to her surprise, her mother agreed to her moving back into the dormitory. In addition to the cramped conditions, there were too many men in the shanty area, and the shanties had to be left open. The camp regulations said only three sides of the shanty could be enclosed, and the interior of the shanties had to be visible from outside. There were no closed doors. It was one thing for her and the little ones, but Emily and Jeannie were grown women whose presence might attract roving eyes. The guards promised not to look, but Margarete didn't trust those promises. Jeannie, too, agreed eagerly to move. As they carried their pitifully few belongings to the dorm, Jeannie whispered, "I saw you talking to Christine. Welcome aboard." Then she walked calmly up the stairs as if she hadn't just dropped a bombshell.

Emily stared after her in shock. Jeannie, who didn't seem to have a serious thought in her head, was involved in this work too? Had, in fact, apparently been involved before Emily herself? Then she realized it was a perfect cover. Who would expect frivolous, empty headed "Jeannie with the light brown hair," as the words of the popular song said, to be involved in counterintelligence?

Resolving not to ask any questions that would put them both in danger, Emily grudgingly developed a new respect for her younger sister. It seemed there were hidden depths to lots of people that only came out in a crisis. As she began to work in the radio group, this principle became more and more apparent. People she had dismissed as silly or uneducated showed up with radio parts at their secret meetings, and a couple of them turned out to have extensive experience in radio, both professional and amateur. Sometimes the "hams," as the amateur radio operators were called, were more knowledgeable about radio than the professionals! They certainly were better at making a radio out of odds and ends, on "chewing gum and baling wire," as the saying went. Emily decided to stop making snap judgments about people, because there might be more to them under the surface.

By the time December rolled around, life in camp had settled into a routine. The anniversary of the attack on Pearl Harbor was a somber event, made worse because the internees didn't dare acknowledge the date openly. There were some snide remarks made by the guards, but as always the internees pretended they didn't understand. They remembered the day in coded remarks with double meanings, and the camp newspaper was a masterpiece of symbolism and veiled allusion.

Former newspaper reporter Beth Harper, of course, was heavily involved in the publication of the camp paper, and in the project to compile as much in the way of news and statistics as possible. The commandant had forbidden keeping diaries, and the daily newspaper was not supposed to comment on camp conditions in any way. Fortunately, the English language is rich enough to allow a wide array of double meanings, and every issue provided a wealth of information for those who could understand the references.

Cultural references to popular songs and books were commonplace-in one instance, the commandant's managing of work details was praised, and the newspaper said he was "as great a leader as our own honored Simon Legree," a reference to the fictional slave overseer in Harriet Beecher's Stowe's novel, Uncle Tom's Cabin. Comic characters, like Li'l Abner and the Katzenjammer Kids, also provided a basis for comparison. Beth insisted these newspaper files would be a valuable record of camp life someday-if they ever got out alive.

Emily's radio work was going forward. She had moved up to coordinator of a small group. They now had three radios in camp, and as group leader, it was her job to get the group together for scheduled meetings, changing the location each time. So far, no one in her group had been caught. One of the members of another group, however, had. Emily still had nightmares about it.

It was a young woman named Peggy. She lived in a shanty, and the guards did a surprise search of the ramshackle structures one day. No one ever knew if it was a random search or if someone had told them they might find something. They found a Morse code key, the piece of equipment used to transmit the sounds of code over the airwaves. She pretended she had found it in the garbage and planned to trade it on the black market for food. She stuck to the story, too, even under torture. Her courage was an inspiration to the others, and she never did incriminate anyone else, even up to the moment she was taken out and shot. Emily would never forget her.

She'd done a lot of growing up in the year since that last party at the Army-Navy club. The idea of going to a restaurant and eating as much as she wanted made her almost faint. The family was trying to make the money stretch, but they were down to the last of their cash and soon would have to give up Margarete's jewelry. Emily had volunteered to contribute her engagement ring, since it was more useful to help feed her family than sitting on her finger. Her mother refused the offer, hoping to save that for a last resort. She said Emily might regret it after the war, and Miltie might not be able to afford another if there were hard economic times. Emily thought that was foolish. It was only some metal and carbon, when you came right down to it. Besides, she might never see Miltie again.

And when she did, would he still want to marry her? She had been known for her elegance, her poise, and her sophistication. People said she walked and dressed like a princess. Not anymore! Her dresses-all three of them-were patched and well worn. Her mother and sisters' wardrobes were in the same condition. Annabelle had outgrown her clothes, and they'd managed to get a couple of yards of fabric, plus needles and thread. Margarete took some lengths out of her full, long skirts and used them, as well, to help make new clothes for her youngest daughter; the old dresses were cut up to make patches for everyone else's clothing.

How strange it seemed to have been worried about the cut of a dress, the kind of embroidery, the fullness of a skirt! Those things didn't matter anymore. Food was a more pressing concern. Little Annabelle hadn't had a cup of milk in more than six months. That wasn't good for growing bones. They were all getting painfully thin. Some people were still eating well, if they had

Filipino friends on the "outside." It was still permissible to have food brought in over the walls. Unfortunately, most of the Coates family's close friends were carefully watched. They were mostly Spanish and German, and while the Japanese didn't consider them "enemy aliens", they were nevertheless under observation and couldn't move as freely as the Filipinos. Also, some of their Filipino friends had moved on to the Coates plantation to try to keep it safe, and they were no longer in Manila-if they were still alive at all. Margarete didn't want to get their Manila friends in trouble, so she was careful about what she asked them to bring in.

There was another factor, one that Emily came at last to understand. Many people in camp didn't have friends in Manila. They had no way to get the extras that some of the well-connected folks took for granted. Margarete believed that it was wrong to cook savory meats-steaks, for example--when most of the people in the camp were living on rice and yams. She bought laying hens, as she had done before, and the family supplemented its diet with eggs and the vegetables from the small plot Margarete planted. The beans still provided most of their protein. At first, Emily thought it was foolish not to use their money to buy good food, but gradually she saw the wisdom of it. They would probably be living with these people for the duration of the war. There was no sense in stirring up envy. They were all prisoners together. By the end of the year, their money was running out even with careful management, and expensive food was not possible for them. The money had to last as long as possible.

Chapter Six

The camp did its best to celebrate Christmas in spite of circumstances. Emily arrived early at the dining hall for the camp Christmas party, and couldn't help remembering celebrations of previous years. She and Jeannie did their best to brighten up their attire with bright red ribbons and bits of borrowed finery. Some of the women had managed to bring gala clothing into camp, and shared it freely. The party was for everyone, including children, and Margarete made sure the younger girls were looking their best. Still, it was a sad occasion under the brittle laughter and song. Internees exchanged handmade gifts, and the meal was as close to a feast as they could make it, with real chicken mixed in with the rice, plus local vegetables and fruits. Everyone had chipped in to buy extras for the meal. It was meager, but it was better than Thanksgiving. Emily still cringed at the memory of a turkey-shaped loaf made of mongo beans. Still, they were alive, and that counted for something.

After the meals and some Christmas carols, the children were sent off to bed, and the adults pushed back the tables for some dancing. The camp orchestra was fairly decent, but Emily just wasn't in the mood for dancing ... not that there were any eligible young men in camp. At this time, it was mainly married men. The cheerful swing music grated on her nerves. She was having a hard time keeping a bright smile pasted on her face. She decided to leave the party early and go back to the dorm. She laid down on her mat and tried to sleep, knowing that she would have to be up early the next morning if she hoped to have a bath. Then she heard footsteps, and someone entered the room.

It was Christine. "I thought I might find you here," she said, coming over to sit on the floor next to Emily's mat.

"What's up?" asked Emily, thinking there was probably going to be a radio team meeting.

"I've got bad news, kid." Christine looked at the floor, clearly at a loss for words.

"Group C just picked it up." The radio groups had been staggering their transmissions so that one of the groups was on the air at least every couple of days. It increased their exposure to information, but also increased the risk. Everyone thought it was worth it.

"What's the news? It must be pretty bad, for you to make a special trip to tell me."

"It is. I don't know how to tell you this, so I'll just say it straight out. Problem is, you can't tell anyone yet, because it's not official."

"I'll keep quiet."

"OK, here it is." Christine took a deep breath. "It's about your father. We got word he was shipped to Japan along with some military prisoners."

"But he's not military!"

"Our little friends didn't believe that, apparently. They classified him as military because he was captured on a military base."

"What was he doing there?"

"Trying to arrange a flight for your family to Singapore on a Brit plane."

Emily shook her head in despair. "That's like Papa. Always thinking of us, and not his personal safety."

"There's more. There's a report that the ship he was on was fired on by our boys. It made it to Japan, but there were a lot of casualties."

Emily turned pale. "No. You're not going to tell me..."

"'Fraid so, kid. The report lists your father as one of the casualties."

"Maybe it's a mistake."

"Anything's possible, but our sources were pretty sure. He was the only civilian, so the others were kind of watching out for him. They knew who he was. Some anti-war Buddhists in Japan got permission to visit the prisoners after the survivors got off the ship, and that's the source of our Intel."

Tears started to run down Emily's face. "What do I tell Mama? She'll fall apart. I just know she will. She's tries to be strong, but I don't know if she can face this." She wiped the tears off-a futile effort, as more continued to run down her cheeks in a steady stream. "I can't tell her. She has enough to cope with. Papa told me to take care of the family. I just can't burden her with this. Besides, what if it turns out it's not true?"

"That's your decision," Christine said softly. "You have to make it yourself. I know what I'd do if I were in your place. I'd keep it quiet. Not just for the reasons you gave, either," she said, as Emily was about to speak. "If your mother lets out that she knows your father's gone, someone will ask where she got that information. It could compromise our security. I'm not saying you can't tell her. I just want you to think about it. If she knows, will she tell the little girls? Will they keep a secret? Maybe the older one, but do you think Annabelle is old enough to be trusted with a life or death secret?"

"You're right. I hadn't thought of that. Annabelle would blab it all over the camp. She's only nine. I guess it's up to me to keep it to myself and just pray it's a ghastly mistake."

"That's the spirit. You just keep on doing what you're doing. You have no idea how important your work is to the war effort. Yes, we're soldiers, too, Emily. We're doing our part. The folks back home are probably doing theirs, too. And, of course, so are the men in uniform, and the nurses. They're the heroes everyone sees, but we have quiet heroes, too, like you and your sister. We all have to pull together. Every little thing we do is part of the overall scheme of things. It all matters. So you go put on some rouge if you have any left, and get back to the party. Dance your heart out as if nothing happened. You don't know anything, right?"

"Right. I'll do it. It won't be easy", she faltered, tears welling up again.

"No, it won't be easy. You can do it, though. I know you can."

Emily washed her face, dug out her last remaining tube of lipstick and applied some to her cheeks, blending it in with some cold cream. When she ran out of cosmetics, she'd have to find some other way to look bright and cheerful, she thought. What did they do before they invented cosmetics? Wasn't that the ancient Egyptians? For a moment, she tried to imagine herself as Queen Nefertiti, trying to deal with the political conflicts of the day. As the wife of the unpopular monotheistic pharaoh, Akhenaton, Nefertiti must have had some interesting struggles to deal with. She was probably glad they had invented cosmetics, too.

Well, thought Emily, if Nefertiti could do it, so can I. I have something she didn't. I have hope. I can count on our boys to get us out of here someday. General McArthur promised to return, and he will, and this will all be over. I can trust in God to keep us safe until then, and I can pray that Papa is really just hiding somewhere and this news is all a mistake. Squaring her shoulders, she left the dorm and returned to the party, determined to show a happy face to the world.

Chapter Seven

January 1943 brought more trouble. Some of the men in camp were found to have been connected to the military. They were moved from Santo Tomas to Fort Santiago. This notorious prison camp was primarily a torture center, and being sent there was almost like a death sentence. As more and more news came in about the treatment of American military prisoners, Emily became convinced that the news of her father's death had some basis in fact. The camps were worse than anyone could have imagined. The civilian camps like Santo Tomas were bad enough. The Japanese, however, were much less brutal to civilians than to the military. They were kindest to the old people, and then to the little children, but they had only scorn for able-bodied men who allowed themselves to be captured.

The warrior ethic of that time demanded fighting to the death, and allowed no possibility of surrender. A soldier who surrendered, or who failed to suicide when captured or hopelessly surrounded, was considered a coward. Civilians were starved and humiliated, but were generally not tortured or physically mistreated unless they gave cause-the kind of thing, Emily realized, that she was doing every day. Harmless civilians generally were safe from physical brutality. This was not the case with soldiers or those men suspected of military ties. They were physically tortured and brutalized on a regular basis, for no reason at all. Prisoners of war who gave any cause whatsoever for retribution were killed without a second thought. And the smallest thing could be considered "cause"-a sneer, failing to bow low enough, fainting in line.

The reports from Cabanatuan prison, where many of the soldiers from the Bataan Death March had been taken, were horrific. Many Filipinos were trying to help them, smuggling in food and medicines, at the risk of their own lives. This risk began to intensify even in the civilian prisons, and people caught trying to help prisoners were tortured or executed.

It was not always the mistreatment by their captors that galled the most. Some within the camp were taking advantage of the situation. A class system was beginning to grow up in the camp, and those with money or credit were still able to buy food through the gate, though the prices were extortionate. Rather than sharing with others, some internees were hoarding food, and flaunting their possessions in front of their less fortunate compatriots. Conflict between the "haves" and the "have-nots" reared its ugly head. Emily's family fell somewhere in between; they had a shanty, but not a lavish one, and their threadbare clothing and meager diet placed them more on the side of the have-nots.

Things were not going well with the Executive Committee. The camp's own internee government began to suffer the inevitable corruption that comes with power. Bribery, long a way of life in euro-colonial Asia, was an established fact. The internee jail served as a way for prisoners to punish their own. The original idea was that if the internees policed their own people, the Japanese wouldn't take on that task, and sentences imposed by Americans were bound to be more humane. This wasn't always the case, especially for those who offended the leaders. They sometimes spent months in the camp jail for minor offenses like drinking alcohol, which was supposed to be prohibited. Guards, of course, drank liquor-especially sake-and favored prisoners were allowed to partake, but the rank and file prisoners were not.

The privileges weren't limited to alcohol consumption. Tobacco was in short supply, and although cigarettes were provided in the Red Cross packages that came in from time to time, these usually went to the guards and the favored few. Not only that, prisoners wondered why some internee leaders-not to mention kitchen workers-weren't losing weight to the degree that most prisoners were doing. These privileged ones even enjoyed the most cherished luxury-unlimited toilet paper.

By spring, toilet paper was strictly rationed in the camp. People were issued four small squares of toilet paper each day. Emily, like many others, tried to find humor in the situation, but it was just another humiliation. Hygiene continued to be a problem, but it was helped by a soap-making plant built by the internees. Now, at least, there was soap, even though it was caustic, lye-based, and strong-smelling.

In late spring, there was more bad news. In May, the commandant announced the camp would be moved to Los Baños, a resort some forty miles outside Manila. The name meant "the baths" in Spanish, but there were no facilities to speak of other than resort cottages. Barracks, dining hall, kitchen, and administrative buildings would all have to be built by the prisoners themselves. This site was considered more defensible, as it was outside Manila and not as easy to escape from. That wasn't the main consideration. As harsh as conditions were, after nearly a year and a half Santo Tomas had become like home. People had their shanties, their vegetable plots, and the whole camp culture. If this move took place, prisoners were told they could only take the clothes on their back. All other possessions had to be left behind.

Fortunately, after considering the economic realities, the Japanese concluded it would be too expensive to move the entire camp. They decided to move most of the men and some of the women-those suspected of potential military connections, like nurses-to Los Baños. Two hundred men volunteered, courageous souls who hoped to spare some of the weaker ones. Six hundred more were drafted. Nearly 800 men and a dozen nurses were moved to Los Baños, with orders to construct barracks and other facilities as soon as possible. There was still a hope that more prisoners could be moved there later.

This relieved the overcrowding, but only briefly. More prisoners were brought in from Manila-dangerous "enemy aliens" like old men, women, and invalids. The oldest was 93 years old-a dangerous fellow, indeed. Soon the camp population was greater than it had been before the move to Los Baños. The resulting change in the camp demographic was startling. With most of the able-bodied men gone, Santo Tomas became a camp run mainly by the women, especially the young and middle-aged women. Free elections, along with attrition, brought about a change in camp leadership, and the tone of the camp became more of a community than the businesslike atmosphere the previous leadership had tried to maintain. Old folks sat in chairs in front of their shanties and traded stories of the "old days," and Santo Tomas began to move at a slower pace.

Not for Emily, however. The radio project became more and more intense. While the guards found no entire radio, they suspected the radios existed, and became ruthless in their frustration. Possession of any kind of electric or electronic material was a capital crime. Even a strand of wire or cable could mean a death sentence. The radio groups had to be extremely careful, and there were some losses-tragic, but unavoidable. Emily became skilled at hiding components, and wished she could do even more for the war effort. She, too, was becoming a soldier-something the Japanese guards never suspected. They had somehow failed to note her employment by the Army Air Corps, something she was sure was a case of miraculous divine intervention in answer to her mother's fervent prayers. They also took no note of her increased self-confidence, since women were mostly insignificant to them, viewed as purely decorative rather than as potential warriors in their own right. Emily's determination increased, and she resolved to be on the lookout for more opportunities.

That was a resolution that served her well before too long. One morning, just at dawn, she ran into a familiar face at the water faucet. Not that this was unusual-by now she knew everyone in camp-but this woman was a few years older, in her early thirties, the oldest daughter of a prominent American family. The Harper family was well known, based primarily in Mindanao, where they had started the Mindanao Herald, the first English newspaper in the islands. Jeannie had briefly dated one of the brothers, and the younger sisters were casual acquaintances. While Emily had known about the older sister before internment, they hadn't moved in quite the same social circles. Nevertheless, she greeted her cheerfully.

"Beth! Fancy meeting you here! Not quite your customary haunts, I'd say," Emily said as she looked around at the dusty grounds, stained walls, and rusted water pipes that provided the décor of the area behind the main building.

"Oh, you know how it is. I think I'll write this joint up for the society page. You mark my word; in no time at all everyone who's anyone will be clamoring to be here." Beth Harper had been the noted society reporter for the Manila Herald, and her descriptions of the fashionable social events of the day had made her a must on any hostess' invitation list. Even in camp, she managed to look professional and stylish, with a Joan Crawford air about her that even the harsh conditions couldn't shake. Somehow, in faded Bermuda shorts and checked shirt, she was clearly someone to be reckoned with.

"It's got a certain charm, don't you think?" Emily finished washing her hair, wrapped it in a threadbare towel, and carefully returned her sliver of harsh, nasty-smelling soap to its tinfoil wrapping as Beth took her place at the relatively odor-free faucet.

"It certainly does. Beats the heck out of the dormitory baths any day. So how are you doing? I see you still have your engagement ring. Haven't sold that yet, obviously. You're one of the few, my dear. Nearly everyone I know would sell off every bit of gold, including the fillings in their teeth, for a can of Spam. You still engaged to that sailor?"

"Lieutenant, not sailor. Far as I know, I am. Haven't heard from him since we got here. I think he shipped out right after Pearl."

"Do the powers that be know the name of your fiancé?"

Emily frowned in puzzlement. "No, why should they? It never came up."

"That's good," said Beth. "You game for a little subterfuge?"

Emily laughed inwardly. As if she weren't practicing a little subterfuge on a daily basis! "Depends what it is."

"Well, this would be a personal favor to me. You know we can't get communication to the other camps, unless it's to someone you're married to, or engaged to."

"So?"

"So my brothers are in Los Baños." A few months after the initial move of prisoners, the other camp was almost completely isolated. They didn't have the help of local residents and couldn't get extra food and materials from outside. No one was really sure what conditions were like there. "Mom would sure like to know how Jimmy and Kells are doing, not to mention the rest of us are also a mite concerned. You interested in helping us? You've got the qualifications."

"What kind of qualifications? What do you think I could do?" Emily knew a moment of fear. Was Beth asking her about her intelligence work? Worse yet, did she know about the radio? She had no reason to think Beth untrustworthy, and yet...

"Your Spanish, of course. You write it like it was your native language. I know you were chummy with that whole upper crust Spanish crowd. I read that piece you wrote in Spanish for the embassy dinner."

What a relief. She didn't know about the radio group, after all! Still, Emily was curious. "I don't get it. What does that have to do with anything?"

"Simple. We need someone who is known to be engaged, and will write letters in Spanish to her fiancé."

"But I don't know where he is. Besides, Miltie doesn't read Spanish!"

"My brother Jimmy does. Pretty darn well, too. Matter of fact, he's written some technical manuals in Spanish." Emily stared at her, still confused. "Don't you see, Em? You pretend you're engaged to Jimmy. Then you can write to him at Los Baños ... in Spanish."

"Why in Spanish?"

"Because the Japanese don't read Spanish too well. They barely decipher English. It should be easy to write some useful information disguised as, say, a love letter, don't you think?"

The light went on. Brilliant, Emily thought. She grinned. This could work well with her other job, and more than double her effectiveness. Just one thing bothered her.

"Will your brother mind getting love letters from someone he hardly even knows? After all, he could get in serious trouble if it got found out. And I've heard that he's an engineer ... they aren't too daring, are they? All those slide rules and everything. Won't he balk at this?"

"Not at all. I know him better than the rest of the family. We went back to the States together for college. He's got guts, I tell you. There's nothing he won't do for our country. You can count on him."

"All right, then, I'm in." For the second time, Emily felt as if she were putting her head into a noose ... all in a good cause.

The next day, she wrote her first letter to James Harper. She'd never actually met him, but of course, the American community knew all about each other. She knew the Harper family by sight, but only the youngest sister, Sheila, was close to her age. Maggie, the other sister, was a good five years older, and although they mixed in the same social circles they had never really gotten to know each other. Kells, the younger brother, was also in their social set, but he had married just before the war broke out. His wife, Frederica, was considered something of a snob, but Emily really didn't know her well enough to form an opinion. She knew James was about a dozen years older than she, and that he had gone to college in the States, but aside from that she knew very little about him. This wasn't going to be an easy task.

"Querida," she began, using the familiar Spanish endearment. She went on in the most flowery terms she could think of, managing to bury a message in with all the sugary love words. Briefly, between the lines, she told him about the plan to write to him, posing as his fiancée, and let him know his mother and sisters were surviving and in good spirits. Then she signed the letter, addressed the envelope, and took it unsealed to the censor's office. The Japanese official perused the letter, nodded knowingly, and let it pass, stamping it with his purple stamp. She had succeeded! So far, anyway.

Chapter Eight

Emily continued her correspondence with James Harper—or, as she now called him, Jimmy--well into the year. It was highly successful. One of the men who set up a radio at Santo Tomas had gone with the first group to Los Baños, and built another radio there. Emily was able to use her letter writing to inform Jimmy of scheduled transmissions from Santo Tomas, and to learn of transmissions from his camp. They were also able to pick up broadcasts from as far away as San Francisco via short wave and rebroadcast these locally, to be picked up on long wave sets. Her "love letters" became an important part of the communications link in the camps.

They were becoming more than that to her, however. This serious-minded engineer who had a strange sense of humor and a taste for adventure was becoming a good friend. She was soon sharing her deepest thoughts and fears with him, including her grief over the probability that her father was dead. Jimmy's father had died before the war, in a house fire, so he knew the pain of loss first hand. Their letters became longer and more frequent.

Emily also found herself involved with another effort-the hospital brigade. Prisoners could be sent to General Hospital in Manila for treatment of serious disorders, and it soon became an avenue for smuggling small items in and out of camp. It was also easier to escape from the hospital than from the camp, and at least one of their radio operatives went to the hospital for a supposed weeklong stay. In reality, he headed for the hills, where he helped them install a radio setup, and returned to camp on schedule without detection. Emily had a less technical but equally vital role; she was bringing information to the underground resistance fighters, many of whom worked at the hospital as a cover for their clandestine activities. This required a major sacrifice on her part--her appendix.

The camp doctor signed a certificate saying she needed an appendectomy, and she went to the hospital. Her healthy appendix was duly removed, and she enjoyed two weeks of halfway decent food and rest while being debriefed by the resistance. She returned to camp with an equal amount of information stored in her head, which she passed on to Christine and others in the camp underground. She, too, had shed blood for the war effort, and her appendectomy scar was as significant and precious to her as any soldier's battle scars and war wounds. It, too, was a souvenir of warfare, and was the mark of a warrior. Emily found it ironic that the Japanese, with their extensive code of bushido, the "way of the warrior," couldn't begin to realize that the half-starved American women they despised were turning into some of the bravest warriors of all.

Shortly after her post-operative return to camp, the Christmas season came around again. This year was particularly bittersweet. A few hundred more internees had gone to Los Baños, but Emily wasn't one of them. Her work was too important, so she didn't volunteer. She considered it, because she was developing a wish to meet Jimmy. She had seen him around town, but until their letters hadn't exchanged more than a word or two, and she had a burning desire to say to him all the things she had been putting down on paper.

It wasn't to be, at least not yet. The new transfers were wives of men already there, or else Roman Catholic priests and nuns and non-Catholic Christian ministers. This left Santo Tomas a little thin of spiritual comfort, but the guards didn't care about that. They wanted the religious folks in one place where they could keep a closer eye on them. The fact that the American prisoners weren't despairing, as they had expected, was peculiar, and they attributed it to the spiritual leadership of these people. These transfers were probably an attempt to weaken the internees' spiritual strength. However, some of Emily's closest friends were among the transferees, and she felt even less like partying than she had last year.

She went to the dorm, got her writing materials, and made a visit to her mother's shanty. It was a pleasant evening, and she planned to sit with Annabelle, who was still a bit too young for an evening party, in Margarete's opinion. Charlie was old enough, and excited about going, so she and her mother went to the party while Emily stayed with her youngest sister.

She was looking forward to the evening. It would be quiet, and she could write a letter to Jimmy. In flawless Spanish, she poured out her heart to a man she didn't really know. "I am getting discouraged," she wrote. "This has gone on so long. It has been nearly two years, and the holiday season is making me realize how much time has passed." She thought carefully about what would get past the censors. Not only did she have to worry about how to frame her coded messages-she also had to be aware that the censors would not let any negative comments about the camp get through. "I grieve that I am separated from those I love, especially at this season. How wonderful it would be to see my loved ones face to face! Memories of other holidays fill my soul. I take comfort in my family, as well as your sisters' presence, but it's not enough. You know the desires of my heart," she said, knowing he would understand she was talking about the end of the war. "I live for the day when those desires will be fulfilled."

As she finished up the letter, her thoughts turned to the coming year. What would 1944 bring? Would she be alive to see another Christmas?

Chapter Nine

Changes began almost at once in the New Year. On January 2, a new batch of prisoners arrived, transferred from another internment camp in Davao. Now there were almost 4,000 prisoners, and the camp facilities and resources were already stretched to the limit. On a more positive note, the radio transmissions brought good news. There had been significant Allied victories in the Pacific, and just knowing about them lifted the internees' spirits. They even were able to receive a short-wave transmission of President Roosevelt's Christmas speech, and made careful copies to distribute throughout the camp. Red Cross packages arrived, containing vitamins, which some prisoners took as an omen that they would survive the year.

Other news was not so good. In mid-January, the camp was transferred from civilian status to military. Knowing the treatment given to military prisoners at Fort Santiago and Cabanatuan, the internees became extremely concerned. Reports of violence and torture at the fort were horrifying. Prisoners were brutally beaten, tortured with burning cigarettes, stabbed with bayonets. There were no toilet facilities, and the cells were like open sewers. Prisoners were not allowed to talk to each other on pain of further beatings and tortures. The idea that these same practices might become the rule at Santo Tomas was frightening.

The food situation got worse. Under the camp's own internee system of government, the food supply was carefully rationed to stretch as much as possible and to avoid real starvation. Food was not plentiful, but so far no one had died of starvation. In late 1943, the internee officials, fearing that shortages were on the horizon, had stockpiled food in the camp warehouses so they could be used if times became worse. With the military in chargë of the food sources, however, the prisoners no longer were able to manage their supply nor its quantity. The beans, rice, corn, and flour the camp had purchased in late 1943 were used and not replaced. Cash payments into the internee treasury were stopped. By

July, the stockpiled dried food was gone. The camp was entirely dependent on what the Japanese army provided, and what they grew in small gardens in the camp. These gardens became much more important than before, since they provided most of the food for the prisoners.

Under this regime, the main food was a weak soup made of rice, green vegetables, and a local fish with a particularly offensive odor. The fish was not fresh to begin with, and the resulting meals were often inedible. By midsummer, even this poor protein source stopped coming in. The last of the canned goods were opened, mostly canned meats. A twelve-ounce can of meat served four people. In one instance, a single can of corned beef was stretched over ten meals for three people. Tiny bits of meat were added to a daily ration of local greens and rice. Prisoners were consuming less than 800 calories a day per person, an amount lower than recommended for extreme weight reduction. Even this meager bit of meat ran out by the end of October, and the many of the prisoners had no more meat after that point.

All there was to eat was the vegetables in the gardens-small garden plots, not farms, to feed the population of what amounted to a small town. There were also chickens and ducks, and before the middle of the year, people began cooking the chickens instead of keeping them as egg-layers. A few hundred ducks flew in to camp on their progress south in the fall, and joined the ducks in the camp pond. Duck soup began to appear on the menu, with duck broth instead of vegetable broth, and occasionally a shred of duck meat in each bowl. Normally, however, breakfast consisted of a ladle full of very watery mush and weak "coffee" made from various kinds of burnt leaves. Lunch was a cup of broth, generally vegetable broth with no meat, and dinner was a ladle of watery stew made of yams, rice, and occasionally a bit of mongo beans. Protein was rare, and there wasn't even enough rice to fill the stomach once a day. The era of starvation had begun.

It was also an era of tightened rule. Instead of the camp being largely run by the internees' own executive committee, administration of the camp passed to a new council under direct

Japanese control. There was more of an effort to run the camp as a prison rather than as a civilian relocation camp. Repression increased on a daily basis. Internees were no longer allowed to use the outside hospital facilities, so that avenue of transferring goods and information was closed.

The sick and wounded in the camp had to be cared for in the camp infirmary, and everything was in short supply. There were few doctors in camp, and not much in the way of medicines and supplies. Beds were scarce. In some cases, patients lay on grass mats on the floor, in conditions that made Margarete shudder. As a trained nurse, she was now working full time in the infirmary, and told Emily she was appalled at the lack of medicines and equipment, and at the Japanese disregard for the internees' health.

"These people are not like the ones who were running the camp in the beginning," she told Emily. "They are not looking at us as civilians. They see us as enemies, and I believe they will soon be treating us as if we had taken up arms against them. I'm afraid of what will come next."

She was right to be afraid. The new commandant ordered the prisoners to take down two walls of each shanty. This left them completely open to view. The guards promised to close their eyes if women were dressing, but this was more of a joke than anything. The women soon became adept at changing under their bed sheets. Several times a day, the guards searched the shanties, still looking for radios. They searched the dormitories, too, but not as thoroughly.

"I wonder why they don't bother us in here as much as they do the people in the shanties," Emily mused to her sister, Jeannie, as they lay awake on their grass mats one hot, humid night.

"I think they don't like the way it smells," said Jeannie, with a giggle. "I know I don't like it, but I have to live here. They don't."

"Maybe they're afraid of the bedbugs," Emily added, as she picked up one of the little insects from the mat and squashed it under her sandal.

"Who ever thought we'd have a reason to be thankful for the stink and the bedbugs?" said Jeannie.

"Things are just upside down here, that's all." Emily knew she and her sister were both thinking about the radio communications group, and all the other work they had done for the underground. Jeannie, too, had gone to the hospital for an appendectomy. That wasn't an option any more, of course, or they would have planned to have their tonsils out next. Stories were coming in about the increased repression in the city of Manila itself, and rumors abounded.

"Did you hear...?" Jeannie began, but Emily silenced her with a gesture. They still couldn't talk freely in the dorms, because internees had been known to sell information to the guards for a little extra food.

Back in the "old days," the sisters had a Spanish friend who was deaf. She could lip-read quite well, but sometimes she needed to have things written down, or given to her in sign language, a system that used some hand gestures for common words and the letters of the manual alphabet for most of what had to be said. Both sisters had learned sign language to talk to her. It became a kind of code for them, and they had used it often on double dates to communicate without their dates knowing what they were saying. As they often did, they began using it now, spelling out some of the words with the manual alphabet and using signs for the rest.

"Mama said there are more cases of beriberi every day," Jeannie signed. "It's very bad." Beriberi was a nutritional deficiency disease that caused muscle tissue to dissolve to liquid and shrink as the body tried to use all its resources to survive. The fluid filled up in lungs and soft tissue, giving a bloated appearance, and sometimes the increased water retention caused a gain in overall weight. It wasn't a real gain, but was a sign that the body was breaking down. People could drown in their own body fluids when the lungs filled up with the liquid.

Emily nodded, and signed back, "I think I'm getting it. My legs are starting to shrink."

"No! You had such nice legs!" Jeannie signed, always thinking about appearances. Emily smiled, realizing that some things would never change. As much as her sister had become a real underground soldier, she still had her superficial moments. Jeannie continued, "I think I'm OK for now. I'm losing weight, but not too much muscle. A lot of people aren't. There are lots of intestinal problems, and some of them need surgery. Mama says the hospital is really full now. They have to do operations without anesthetic. Sometimes they don't even have clean bandages."

"How sad it is, that people might die because we don't have clean bandages," Emily signed back. "Maybe this will be over soon. Look what I found today. It was dropped by a plane." She handed a plain, cardboard book of matches to Jeannie. It had words printed on the inside: "I shall return." They knew this was the promise General MacArthur had made to the Philippines when he left. Did this mean the Allies were on their way?

It seemed so. The military restrictions were increasing. Even though the Geneva Convention forbade using civilian prisoners for forced labor, it was happening at Santo Tomas. The prisoners were being forced to work from four to six hours a day at various jobs for the Japanese-building a huge bamboo fence around the entire campus, clearing out the perimeter of the camp, and moving shanties fifty feet away from the walls. They also had to dig trenches in case of an air raid, and all this hard labor was even more difficult on a starvation diet.

Some men had lost as much as a hundred pounds over the last year, and most women had lost at least 40. Few women now weighed over 100 pounds. Margarete, along with other nurses and doctors, had tried to persuade the Japanese that this weight loss indicated the prisoners were being starved-also a violation of the Geneva Convention-but they refused to believe it, saying the Americans were too fat before. Worse yet, the children were put on half rations, receiving half of the little amount the adults were getting--around 400 calories a day. The medical personnel tried to explain that children needed more food than the adults, not less, but their pleas were ignored.

In spite of all this, there was good news. Emily shared some of this with Jeannie, whose underground work was in different groups than hers. "War news," she signed, and Jeannie positioned herself on her mat so that no one else could even see the signs Emily was making.

"The Allies have reached Paris," she signed. "Our boys are in the thick of it. It was a combined force with the Brits and the Free French. The Germans are being beaten back. Paris is liberated!"

"Wonderful!" Jeannie spelled. They received no official news of Allied victories. Even when the Allies invaded Normandy, the Japanese only told them that the Germans had attacked Allied forces in Normandy, and implied that it was a great German victory. No word of the American and British being part of an invasion, but that was to be expected. They would probably say nothing about the liberation of Paris, either. Jeannie knew Emily would not pass on this news unless it was well documented and verified by radio.

"What about here in the Pacific?" she asked.

"Very good news," Emily signed. They already knew about the Allied successes in the Marianas, the Solomon Islands, and many other islands across the Pacific. "Guam is ours," she signed, "And FDR is in Hawaii."

"So close!" Jeannie signed. "Why is he there?"

"My sources say they had a big meeting about us!"

"Us? What do you mean? We don't even know the President!"

"Not us as in you and me, silly," Emily signed, giggling. "Us as in the Philippines. The Navy wants to bypass us and go on to Japan, but MacArthur promised to come back, and the radio reports say that FDR approved it."

"So the army really is coming back?"

"Yes, and soon, if MacArthur has his way."

"I tell you, I'm sorry I ever dated those Navy men if this is the way they are going to treat American prisoners of war." Jeannie had the ability to bring every worldwide event down to her personal level. Sometimes Emily admired that, but right now it annoyed her.

"It's not their fault, Jeannie. It's the high brass. They don't know what we're going through. But I have confidence in the

General. He'll be back, just as he promised. Mama always said he was a man of integrity."

"When will he be here?"

"The reports didn't say. I'd guess in the next couple of months."

"That's good," signed Jeannie. 'With any luck, we'll still be alive and won't have died of starvation when he gets here."

Chapter Ten

The next couple of months were a time of anxious waiting. Thanks to the reports coming in through the radio network, most of the prisoners knew the Allies were on their way. It helped keep their spirits up during the increasingly hard times. Hunger was an everyday presence, and the older people were starting to die of starvation. Some of the children died, too. There was no room in the hospital for the dying, so they died in their beds. This made the reality of death all too vivid, even for the little ones. Some small children refused to take the extra food their parents tried to give them, insisting their parents eat it; they were more afraid of their parents' death than of their own.

Repression increased, with offenses such as not bowing to a soldier earning a death sentence. September and early October brought repeated air raids, and prisoners tried not to cheer openly as Allied planes flew overhead. One of them dropped flyers with General MacArthur's picture on it, which the Japanese promptly confiscated. On October

20, the best news of all came over the radio. MacArthur had returned. The Sixth Army landed in Leyte and was advancing towards Manila. The Japanese moved troops in position to repel the assault. Every day, the news was more and more positive. Prisoners began to hope they would get out of camp alive, after all.

The official word in camp made no mention of this, but security tightened still further. Even when local merchants and charity groups tried to bring in food for the prisoners, the Japanese refused, saying the camp had enough food. They didn't want to take the chance of letting in any outsiders who might give good news to the prisoners. As much as possible, they were completely cut off.

The letters to and from Los Baños had stopped earlier in the year, and the radio network was the only source of outside information. Possession of a Manila newspaper earned at least a jail sentence in the military jail, if not also a beating. Clearly, the Japanese didn't want the prisoners to know what was going on in the outside world. Emily found that encouraging.

The radio group found it more difficult to meet. The camp's military rule brought unanticipated problems. Prisoners were expected to work every day at tasks assigned by the captors, in addition to their own camp jobs. Hard, physical labor was mostly what they assigned. The process of digging ditches and clearing the perimeter continued, showing the depth of the enemy's fear of attack.

Prisoners tried to keep their spirits up with group activities, evening entertainment programs, and organized games, but, as Charlotte said, "It's hard to be cheerful when you're starving." Her pessimistic attitude broke Emily's heart. Her younger sister had always been the family "Pollyanna", finding something to be glad about in everything. Not so anymore; the once-perky, optimistic teenager had lost her positive outlook and seemed focused entirely on her own misery.

Just a few months earlier she had moved into the dormitory, along with her mother and little sister. Their shanty had been destroyed in the perimeter-clearing efforts, and they hadn't had enough wood to rebuild it. In some cases, the sturdier buildings had been moved intact to new locations, but theirs wasn't one that survived the move, so they were crowded into the women's dorm along with nearly a thousand others.

Charlie hadn't changed in one important way; she still wanted to join the WAVES or WACs (Women's Army Corps) as soon as they were liberated. At seventeen, she was old enough to join, and reminded her mother of that fact on an almost daily basis. A desire for revenge filled her heart, and with the blind rage of the young she used every hardship to fuel her hate. Every paltry excuse for a meal stirred up the flame of her anger. Margarete tried to talk to her, but she didn't want to listen. She wanted to be angry.

"Mama, you're not going to change her mind," Emily told her one evening in early January. She and her mother were taking a quiet moment to talk. They had brought their mats out on to the balcony of the second floor dormitory and were enjoying the relative coolness after the sun went down.

Jeannie and the younger ones were at the Three Kings party, a Spanish custom popular in the Philippines. It was a celebration of the visit of the Magi, and in Spanish and Filipino culture was more of a celebration than Christmas. The Christmas party had been a brave effort, but with nothing resembling a Christmas dinner or merriment, was more a time of sadness than anything. This holiday, on the other hand, didn't trigger so many memories for the Americans and was easier to celebrate without overwhelming grief. Emily pleaded a headache as her excuse for missing the festivities. In reality, she had a radio group meeting in about an hour and wanted some quiet time. Worried, her mother came to see her, and they fell into conversation.

"Emily, I just don't understand that girl. I did not raise you to be filled with hate. That's not our way, daughter."

Emily laughed. "Mama, sometimes I think you're as much of a Quaker as Papa." The memory of her father-and the secret of his death that she was still hiding in her heart-raised a lump in her throat, and she fought back tears.

Margarete understood. "I know, dear. I suppose after many years of marriage, people grow more alike. But all Christians should try not to hate. That's not just for Quakers. Hate destroys the one who hates even more than the one who is hated. Surely you know that."

"Yes, Mama, I do. I understand that these people are trying to win a war, and they're losing it. I think they know that. They're losing battles all over the Pacific, and now that MacArthur's back, they know they'll lose the Philippines, too. I think it's just a matter of days."

"So the war is really going well for the Allies, dear?"

"Yes, it is, Mama. I know you don't like to ask about the news I hear on the radio, but I think you'd be encouraged. We've won many important battles, and the Sixth Army has landed. They're fighting on land; we have control of Leyte, and the last I heard MacArthur had ordered the troops to make the capture of Manila the highest priority. Any day now they'll be in Luzon. Our boys are here, Mama, and ships are moving towards Manila Bay. The aircraft carriers are coming with planes and bombs. It won't be long before we're free."

"But the war will still be going on. We aren't the only ones at risk, Emily. Think of your Papa. We aren't even sure where he is!"

"But, Mama, when we're out of this prison, we can start looking for him. I know we'll get news of him soon."

"I never thought I'd be glad you've been involved in this radio activity of yours, but it's good to know freedom is at hand. I've been so worried about you, but I know you're doing what you feel you must."

"That's right, Mama. I guess in my own way I'm as determined as Charlie to fight back. I just do it in a different way."

Margarete smiled. "It's certainly more ladylike than putting on a uniform and going off to battle, the way Charlie wants to," she said. "You're still a fighter, child. You know I don't believe in violence. I never have. That was one reason I married your father. He also believed as I do, that violence is not the answer."

"Mama, he served in the Army."

"Yes, he did, but he never fired a weapon. He did administrative work for General Pershing. He didn't lack courage, but he deeply believed it was wrong to kill another human being, no matter what the reason. He wanted to support his country, and this was a way he could stay true to his principles and still support what he believed was a good cause. Some of his Quaker associates felt even that was wrong, but your Papa is a very practical man. I'm sure he has also been doing something to help us in this war, even though I'm also certain he would never harm another human being."

"I love the story of how you met. Tell me again, Mama. I need to hear something happy right now."

Margarete laughed. Laughter was such a rare sound; it lifted Emily's spirits immediately. If her mother could still laugh, things couldn't be all bad.

"I've told you that story hundreds of times, and you still ask for it, just as you did when you were a little girl."

"Please, Mama. For a Three Kings gift?" The family had so many Spanish friends that they'd begun years ago to take part in Spanish celebrations. When Emily was a child, they gave each other gifts on Three Kings, and although that custom had faded when the children grew up, she still remembered it fondly.

"Very well; for Three Kings, then. I was seventeen, and I was on a ship going from Jolo to Manila to go to school. My father had died a few months earlier, and I was traveling alone. I was still very upset about his death, and the doctors convinced my mother I would do well to go away to college, so your grandmother enrolled me in a program that combined a teaching course with a degree in nursing. She believed that I should be prepared to earn a living if it became necessary. You know, of course, what happened to the family fortune after my father's death."

Emily nodded. The whole family knew the story of how her grandfather's business partner--a distant relative--had embezzled the family funds, although no one could ever prove it in court. Emily had enough proof for her own certainty, since she had seen one of

115

her grandmother's necklaces adorning the business partner's daughter at a Manila society party before the war. She had come home seething with anger and reported it to her mother. However, Margarete didn't believe in revenge, and strictly ordered Emily to tell no one else.

"So, because there was so little money to live on, my mother believed at least one of her two daughters should be self-sufficient. She was a modern woman who believed women should be trained for a career."

"That's so strange. I don't understand how she ever developed those ideas. After all, her family was Muslim."

"She was raised to value learning. She had no brothers, so her father taught her to read and write-in Arabic, of course-so she could read the Koran. Although she had no formal schooling, just the freedom of learning to read gave her a taste for more learning, and she learned to read and write in German as well. Then, when she married my father, he encouraged her to keep reading. He told her that German girls were allowed to go to school, and she was so thrilled with that idea that she was almost obsessed with the notion that at least one of her daughters would actually go to college. I was chosen, because my sister was not well."

Emily nodded. She had been named after her mother's beloved sister, who died young.

"And so, at seventeen, I sailed for Manila for four years of schooling. I was excited, but a little afraid. I never liked boats, and the weather was very bad. We were caught in a monsoon, and the passengers were tied to the deck so we wouldn't be swept overboard. Finally, after hours of fighting the storm, the ship went down. There were barely enough lifeboats, and there were so many of us packed into that tiny boat I thought we would surely sink. I was terrified, Emily, even more than I have been during this war. I think that experience has made me so calm I can endure anything."

"I can only imagine what it was like, Mama. The monsoons are bad enough on land, nice and secure in a house." Emily didn't add that seeing her father killed before her eyes had probably contributed to her mother's ability to endure horrific experiences without flinching. Even now, Margarete didn't like to talk about her father's death. She continued telling her story.

"The storm finally ended, and we drifted for hours. We had no paddles. Somehow, they had been lost in the storm. I think the other lifeboats were able to row to land, but we drifted further out to sea. Then we saw a ship, and I took off my petticoat and waved it like a flag."

"Mama! How immodest!" Emily said, giggling.

"I was desperate," her mother said calmly. "I would never show my petticoat unless it was a matter of life and death."

Emily knew that was true. During the 1920s, her mother had clung stubbornly to her long skirts, ignoring the fashions of the day, and didn't even allow her young daughters to wear the above-the-knee skirts their friends were wearing. Emily had never worn a skirt shorter than the knee, and even her tennis dresses were much more modest than her friends'. She and Jeannie grumbled, but went along with their mother's notions of modesty.

In camp, she and her sisters occasionally wore Bermuda shorts in the dorm, but her mother refused to wear anything shorter than six inches above the ankle, and wouldn't wear trousers. She dressed like a lady, even in prison camp.

Margarete went on with her story. "The ship came closer, and it turned out it was a small fishing vessel taking your father and a couple of other Americans on a tour of the islands. They saw the petticoat, and they rescued us. I thought your father was the handsomest man I'd even seen, but of course we hadn't been introduced, so I couldn't really get in conversation with him. He tried to find out who I was, and finally I told him my name and said he could write to me at school. Of course, I told my mother he was writing to me."

"Of course, Mama."

"Then, when I graduated, he sent me flowers. He continued to call on me, and although I had other suitors, I still found him the most attractive. Also, as I said, we shared a belief in the evil of war and violence."

Emily nodded. Her mother had learned at an early age about the horrors of violence.

"Mama, I think that's so romantic," she murmured. "Stories like that just don't happen anymore."

"No? What about your young man?"

She gave her mother a puzzled look. "Who are you talking about, Mama?"

"Your fiancé, of course, dear. The lieutenant, Washboard or whatever his name is."

"Washburn. And, Mama, I haven't even thought of him in months. Maybe years. That just seems unreal. That whole world of dances and nice clothes-was it ever real? Did we just imagine it?"

"No, we didn't imagine it. Was it real? Yes, it was, and it was also unreal. It was a kind of illusion, but that doesn't mean it was any more an illusion than this life we're living now. That was a nice illusion, and this is a nasty illusion, but neither of them is entirely real."

This was getting too metaphysical for Emily. "I don't understand, Mama."

"Emily, everything that happens to us can be looked at in different ways. We don't see the whole picture. It's as if we're looking at the back of a tapestry or a piece of embroidery. Our lives are like that. There are all these tangled threads, and some of them don't look very nice. That's because we're looking at it from the wrong side."

"How do we get to look at it the right way, Mama?"

"We do that by faith. We know that all things work together for good, for those who love God and are called to His purpose."

"That's somewhere in St. Paul's letter to the Romans, isn't it?"

"Good, you still remember something from Sunday school. Yes, and I find that verse very comforting these days. We aren't seeing the whole picture. Our lives will never be the same, even when we are out of this place. That way of life-that particular illusion-is gone. But that may be for our good. Maybe we were becoming too fond of the illusion. We were privileged, Emily. We had a life that very few people on this earth can ever know. Even now, back in America, people don't live as lavishly as we did then. Oh, I know you didn't think it was so lavish, but it was. We had some difficult years, but through it all, we managed to have a lovely home, enough food, and a household full of servants. Do you know that in America, most people don't have servants?" Emily nodded, and her mother continued.

"We lived like royalty, and that had to end. We might have begun to think we were better than other people. That's what this war is all about. Some people think they're better than others, and think they have a right to rule the world. That's the problem with this terrible Hitler, who will make the German people a symbol of evil for generations. Because he thinks he has a right to rule the world, he has seduced my father's people into a great and terrible evil. The Japanese, also, have been beguiled by their Emperor, who they think is the descendant of the gods. They think they have the right to rule the entire Pacific, and even the entire world, because the Emperor is divine. That's a great temptation, to think oneself better than others. This has been a hard lesson, but I think that many years from now, although we might feel nostalgia for the 'old days,' we will see that the picture on the front of the tapestry is beautiful."

"Mama, you're a philosopher."

"No, child. I'm just a mother. Now, let's talk about this young man you've forgotten. What will you do after the war?"

"If he's still alive, you mean? I can't give him back his ring. That went for a sack of mongo beans, remember? But I'll have to tell him it just won't work."

"Is there someone else?"

"Not really, Mama. I guess this war has changed me. I don't think the most important thing about a man is whether he's a good dancer or a snappy dresser. I think character is what matters. I can't imagine Miltie dealing with being in prison camp. He was a good officer, but..."

"I understand. I've been concerned about that, myself. I remember his complaints one evening when he came to dinner. The coffee was cold, and he was impatient with the maids, saying it was their fault. That disturbed me."

Emily sighed. "I know. I guess I just didn't want to look at the situation too closely. His family back in the States is wealthy, and he just didn't handle hardship too well. The only good thing about that relationship is that bag of mongo beans!"

"Have you met any men who are men of character?"

"Of course, Mama. This war had brought out the best, as well as the worst, in everybody. But no one really appeals to me in that way."

"What about that fellow you were writing to?"

"Jimmy? He's just a friend, Mama. I've only seen his face once or twice, and that was when he was going out with Jeannie. She didn't like him. She said he laughed at her and was always making jokes. He still does. He always puts something funny in his letters. It doesn't bother me, though. In fact, I think I like it."

"What about his character?"

"Mama, he seems to be a man you could trust. He's very generous, and in all his letters, his foremost concern is for other people, not for himself. I think I'd like to get to know him better after the war."

"That's good enough. Maybe this letter writing will be another thread in the tapestry."

"Or maybe not. Who can say? Right now, I have to go listen to the radio. Maybe there'll be something by Benny Goodman on it!" she said, jokingly. Her mother knew they wouldn't be listening for music.

"Run along, dear. Let me know if there is any news I should know about. I'll go back to the party and join your sisters."

"Yes, Mama. Good night," Emily said, as she picked up her mat and left the balcony.

Chapter Eleven

The group was already assembled when Emily arrived in the laundry room with her radio parts. The radio was almost put together. Silently, she handed over her part to the engineer in charge, and within minutes, the radio was warming up. Group members took turns standing guard to make sure no one was nearby. Few people did laundry late at night. Although the work involved was heavy, and it would have been more pleasant to work after the sun went down, the hard labor during the day left the prisoners exhausted by evening.

Tonight was particularly safe, because of the party. Still, they needed to be careful. The risk of being caught was still there, and the penalty was instant death-for all of them, and also for their families. The military regime brought in the idea of "family dishonor," and if one family member was caught in some forbidden activity, the entire family suffered the same fate as the offender. Emily was much less worried about her own safety than she was about what would happen to her family if she were caught. Nevertheless, she continued in the radio group. The task was too important to run away from.

This time, it was no short wave broadcast they picked up. This was a transmission on the amateur, or "ham", radio band. The groups rotated the frequencies they monitored, and tonight Emily's group was working the ham wavelengths. One member of their group held an amateur radio operator's license, and although the lack of a license was the least of their worries, it pleased them to comply with American regulations. It reminded them that Americans were a people of laws, not criminals, and that flaunting the enemy's rules did not mean they had no respect for law. They had the utmost respect for their own laws-although not necessarily for the enemy's. There was a difference.

"K9VY, W6DB", the voice said, naming the call sign of the camp's radio operator and then his own call sign.

"This is K9VY," their man replied. "How ya doing, Joe?" Emily realized the man's name might not really be Joe; however, he was probably a "G.I. Joe," a soldier.

"Can't complain, Tom. Got some sweet accommodations here. The mud's really fresh tonight, and the mosquitoes aren't too hungry. It just doesn't get any better. How are your folks holding up?"

"Mighty hungry, Joe. Mighty hungry. You think you and your friends might be coming for a visit anytime soon?"

"Matter of fact, we just might do that. Be sure to put the coffee on for us, Tom. We'll be ready to party."

"You planning to visit our buddies in the south?" Tom asked, meaning the camp at Los Baños.

"Sure thing. That's on the agenda. We have to make it fast, though. The word is that their hosts are planning something pretty nasty. We hear they want to have a necktie party for all our buddies on the twenty-fourth of next month. I don't think we want that to happen. Doesn't sound like fun to me."

"Me neither. Any parties like that in the works for us here?"

"Not sure. Rumor is yes, but it's not confirmed. The other guys have written invitations."

Tom gave a low whistle. "That's not good, Joe."

"Dang right. We're doing our best, pal. You tell everyone to hang on and keep their chins up. Uncle Sam is proud of them. We haven't forgotten. That's orders from the top."

"Will do, friend."

"Just a word. Stay clear of the gates and walls. Tell everyone, especially the kids. Lay low as much as you can for the next few weeks. We'll come to see you as soon as we can, and then we'll get our friends in the south."

"Want us to tell them to expect you?"

"Yep. They need to know. See if you can manage something low key. I haven't been able to reach them."

"Thanks for the scoop. W6DB, this is K9VY clear."

"W6DB clear."

The radioman continued to monitor the frequency, changing every minute or so to other frequencies, but there was nothing else to hear. After about twenty minutes, they turned off the radio and took it apart again, handing out the parts to each member, who in turn quietly slipped out to replace the part in its hiding place.

Emily's brain was in turmoil. She understood the message. A "necktie party" was slang from old Western movies--a hanging, and by extension, an execution. The Japanese had written orders to execute all the prisoners in Los Baños on February 24th! The G.I. implied there was a rumor that similar orders had been issued for Santo Tomas, but couldn't confirm it. He also wanted them to warn the prisoners at the other camp, so they would be prepared. What else had he said? Stay away from the gates and walls? That must mean they were planning a land-based attack. Had they landed tanks and heavy artillery? It must be. This was not going to be an air strike. The Army was coming in by land, with equipment to break down walls. She needed to let her mother know, and they all needed to stay close to the center of camp, as the G.I. requested.

What about the problem of notifying Los Baños? Emily realized their radio must not be working, if the G.I. couldn't reach them. They had suffered even more oppression than Santo Tomas, and had less food. Was Jimmy involved with the radio communications in his camp? She didn't know. She also didn't know if there was a chance that she could get a message through to him. The camp commandant had cut off letters between the camps, but maybe she could persuade them to let one little letter get through.

Back in her dormitory, she put together a short letter. "Dear one," she wrote in Spanish, "On this special holiday, I wanted to write to you for your birthday, which is coming up just ten days after Valentine's Day, the day of love and romance. This day makes me think of the famous event in Chicago on Valentine's Day, which celebrated the affection between your friend Al and the one he loved so much. You must know that I am thinking about that famous Valentine's Day as I contemplate your birthday, and hope you understand my thoughts are with you. Take care of yourself, my beloved, until we meet again." Emily knew Jimmy's birthday was in May, and she was sure he would understand this was not a real birthday letter. The Valentine's Day Massacre, in which mobster Al Capone murdered many of his enemies on February 14, 1929, was something she knew he would know about. He had been in America going to college when that happened. He wouldn't miss the reference, and would know some kind of massacre was planned for the 24th of February, ten days after Valentine's Day. Between the fact that it was written in Spanish and carried cultural references she hoped the Japanese wouldn't understand, there was a good chance it would pass censorship. Now, if only she could get the commandant to allow the message to go through!

Emily decided to take a dangerous step. The next morning, she went to the commandant. She dressed very modestly, because she had heard the commandant was offended by immodest dress on women. Also, she knew the guards were not always polite to women who were wearing tight or skimpy clothing. She bowed properly, as the guards had taught them, though she hated having to do it. Calmly, she made her request.

"Honorable commandant," she said, "I know you are a person of great discernment. I ask your permission to send this letter to my fiancé in Los Baños. His birthday is in a few weeks, and I would like him to receive a greeting in my own hand."

The commandant took the letter and tried to read it. "What language is this?"

"Spanish, sir. My fiancé doesn't speak English very well."

"Is he not an American?"

"Yes, sir, because his father was American, but his mother is Spanish and they always spoke Spanish at home." Emily couldn't believe she was lying so calmly-and, she hoped, convincingly. In reality, she knew Mrs. Harper, Jimmy's mother, wasn't Spanish; Emily didn't think she even spoke a word of that language. Still, she hoped it would work.

Apparently, it had. The commandant shrugged, and said, "I will approve this on one condition. You must write me a statement saying I am kind and merciful to prisoners, and sign it with your own name. You must also tell all the other prisoners of my kindness, and tell them they must be polite and respectful to me, with proper bowing and respectful attitudes."

Emily agreed eagerly, and handed him the envelope addressed to "Señor Diego Harper." Diego was one of the Spanish equivalents of James, and she always addressed her letters to him that way. The commandant looked at the envelope, grunted, and folded her letter, putting it in the envelope. He sealed it and stamped it with his approval, then gave it to his aide and said something to him in Japanese. The aide bowed, took the envelope, and left the room.

As Emily walked back to her work station, she hoped the letter would find its way to Jimmy. At least, if he knew this execution was planned, he would be watchful. In case the Sixth Army didn't arrive in time, the prisoners in Los Baños would be warned of their danger. It was a long shot, but it might work. Also, there was the spiritual consideration. People deserved to have enough warning to prepare themselves emotionally and spiritually for death. That was allowed to condemned criminals; surely, it was also something these innocent civilians deserved!

The next few weeks passed in a fog. The food supply dwindled even more, and everyone was lightheaded. It was hard to do even light work, and the heavy labor the Japanese demanded was impossible. People were fainting on the job, and even more were dying of starvation. The prisoners hung on to the hope that they would soon be rescued, but as each day passed the hope became weaker. Where was the U. S. Army?

The radio broadcasts from military sources had come to a halt. Emily figured the army was too busy fighting to get on the air. Some snippets of news got through, however, broadcast by Filipino civilians. On January 24, the U. S. captured Clark Field, a former U. S. airfield that was now the main Japanese airbase in the Philippines. This news was wonderful, and as it was whispered through the camp, Emily saw eyes sparkling with excitement. Rescue couldn't be too far away!

On the first of February, U. S. forces landed just southwest of Manila. The battle for the capital city was about to begin. The commandant and the guards were even stricter, ready to shoot anyone they considered a threat. They were packing up, shredding and burning documents, and as she saw smoke rising from the incinerator drums filled with official paper, Emily realized the Japanese were expecting to leave camp in a hurry. She became convinced they would kill all the prisoners. Had Jimmy gotten her message? Was he prepared?

In her worry, she turned more and more to prayer. She remembered the story she had heard about Patrick, the favorite saint of Ireland. Yes, he was known for using the example of a shamrock to illustrate the concept of the Trinity, but there was more. There was the story of his journey to talk with the King of Ireland, and along the way encountering some enemies. According to the legend, when they passed by, the enemies only saw a flock of deer, and they continued their journey safely.

As she thought about the danger she was in, praying for the same kind of safety and protection, she seemed to see the power of her enemies diminish. She could almost imagine that if they looked at her, they would see only a deer—or, considering the location, perhaps a chicken. They way she had been protected throughout the years of captivity made it seem as if she had sometimes been invisible. When she crept from one hiding place to another, went to clandestine radio meetings, and even when she went to the commandant to get him to send her letter, she had often felt an unearthly sense of strength. In the midst of her enemies, there was peace, and incredible blessings.

One blessing was that, in the confusion of preparing to evacuate, the Japanese were no longer assigning the prisoners to hard labor. Tired, starving, the prisoners lay around during the day, trying to conserve what little energy they had. They told stories, often retelling from memory tales from books they had enjoyed as children, books that either had never made it into camp or been sold long ago for a scrap of food. To keep fit, they tried to exercise, but most couldn't manage more than a few minutes' slow walk around the grounds- always trying to keep clear of the walls, not only because of Japanese regulations but also because of "G. I. Joe's" warning, which had been passed around through the camp.

The Japanese were pleased that, for some reason, the prisoners were being remarkably obedient about following regulations, especially concerning keeping the perimeter clear. Not one prisoner broke the rules by trying to get too close to the walls. The guards attributed it to their excellent management, of course, as they relaxed a bit and put their attention on destroying any documents or evidence that might be used against them in a war crimes trial. The commandant knew this might be a possibility, and asked many prisoners for letters attesting to his kindness and mercy. Most complied; they knew it wouldn't matter in the long run, once the U. S. Army arrived. At this point, they just wanted to survive long enough to see the day of their rescue.

One morning in early February, Emily woke later than usual. The dormitory was deserted. She realized she had slept through breakfast; should she hurry and get dressed? Breakfast, these days, was weak tea or fake coffee made from roasted roots. Sometimes there was a watery porridge or gruel, but most mornings it was just the tea or "coffee", usually without milk or sugar. That didn't seem worth going to the dining hall for.

However, the shower room was also empty; Emily decided to take advantage of the opportunity to have a shower in peace and quiet. She grabbed her threadbare kimono, patched in several places, and a scrap of towel and sliver of soap. She walked slowly to the shower room-she had no energy for moving quickly. Taking a shower all by herself was a luxury she cherished, and not having to hurry and get out of the way for the hundreds who were waiting was also a delight. She took her time with the shower, washed her hair, dried off and put on her kimono. Slipping in to her native sandals, she returned to the dormitory, expecting to see it filled with women who had come back from breakfast. There was no one there.

Suddenly, Emily was frightened. Where was everyone? There was a hush over all the camp-a deadly silence. Had they taken everyone out after breakfast and shot them?

Or poisoned them, perhaps in their food or drink? The last few days the guards had often forgotten about roll call, but perhaps they had done that today. Was she the only one left? Had they noted her absence and were now coming to kill her? How terrible to be the only one left alive! What had happed to her mother and sisters? If they were gone, she wanted to die with them.

Frantic, panicky, she ran down the stairs, tying her kimono around her as she ran, her sandals clattering on the floor. She heard a rumble outside, and gunfire. What was happening? Terrified, she ran out the front door of the main building, just as a huge tank crashed through the front gate.

The gate toppled; the tank rode over it and stopped right in the middle of the grounds. Dumbfounded, Emily saw the Stars and Stripes painted on the side of the vehicle. It was an American tank! The Sixth Army had arrived! She raced towards the tank, not caring if there was any danger. The top of the tank opened, and a dirty, dusty soldier climbed out as more troops came in through the open gates.

Now, Emily saw the rest of the prisoners. They, like her, were running towards the soldiers. Emily ran up to the soldier and wrapped him up in a big hug. "Thank you!" she said over and over again, tears streaming down her face.

"You'd better get back inside, ma'am. There might be some fighting," the soldier said in a decidedly southern American accent. Emily wiped the tears off her face and re-entered the dormitory, along with hundreds of other women. Everyone was crying. They went upstairs and crowded on to the second-floor balcony, where they had a good view of the most beautiful sight in the world.

The flag of Imperial Japan, the Rising Sun, with all its arrogance and pride, came down and lay forgotten on the dirt, as the Star Spangled Banner rose in its stead. Some soprano voice rang out, "Oh, say can you see ..." and it seemed to Emily that the whole camp joined in with one voice, singing their hearts out for this beloved emblem of the land of the free and the home of the brave.

Chapter Twelve

There was no fighting in the camp itself. The commandant and guards had all left in the early hours, probably right after dawn. It turned out no one had seen them at breakfast, and the kitchen staff took the opportunity to make sure everyone had a half-scoop of watery porridge and some sugar. Emily had missed the biggest breakfast the camp had enjoyed in weeks. She didn't care; she had welcomed the U. S. Army without the usual dirt of the camp, and felt it was worth it.

The soldiers had come prepared with Red Cross food packets, and distributed chocolate bars to the starving prisoners. There wasn't enough for everyone to have a whole chocolate bar, but nearly everyone got a small square or two, and the soldiers brought flour, lard, and sugar into the kitchens, where the kitchen staff eagerly stirred up biscuits and cookies. In the meantime, the soldiers helped "liberate" the supplies the Japanese had hidden away, revealing rice, beans, and canned meats that fed the prisoners generously for days. There was much more foods than they were used to, and some prisoners became ill before the medical staff told them to take it easy and slowly work back up to normal eating.

Fighting continued in Manila, however. The liberated prisoners were free to go around the city, and in the next few days, the air war had reached the city. Bombs were falling all around, but they scarcely noticed. Emily and Jeannie walked around the city in a state of shock. They could hardly believe they were free!

At a food vendor's stall, they overheard an American in uniform, wearing sergeant's stripes, trying to buy some food. He had no idea what to buy. The girls stopped and helped him, and Emily thought she recognized his voice. Taking a guess, she asked, "Are you W6DB?"

"You betcha," he answered. Name's Bob Francis, from California. Who are you lovely ladies?"

They introduced themselves, and Bob was clearly taken with Jeannie. Emily explained that she recognized his voice from the radio, and told him about her work. Bob was impressed, but much more impressed with Jeannie, who didn't even flinch when bombs fell less than a block away.

"You're the bravest woman I ever saw," he said, awestruck.

Emily stifled a giggle. She wasn't about to tell this soldier that her sister was just in a state of shock, barely aware of the bombs at all. Let him think it was courage, if he wanted. Everyone was entitled to some illusions.

Bob had a few hours' leave, and the girls walked around town with him for a while. He was an amateur radio operator-a "ham"-as Emily already knew. He came from a small town on the central California coast, and spent much of the time talking about his hometown and its beautiful scenery.

Jeannie expressed a wish to see the beautiful beaches he described. Emily found this amusing; they had grown up a stone's throw from the beach on the family plantation in Sulu. It was clear the tall G.I. was the real attraction, not the California beaches, but Emily didn't want to stop their fun.

Finally, it was time for Bob to rejoin his unit. As he was about to leave, Emily decided to ask the question that had been troubling her. She knew he might not be able to answer, due to security policies, but she asked anyway.

"What about Los Baños? Are they going to be rescued in time?"

"Definitely. We came to San Tomas first because we had a pretty reliable rumor that the Japanese were deserting the camp, and that they were planning to bomb it with all the prisoners inside. We have another unit already on its way to Los Baños. They're working their way to the camp. The guards there haven't left, and I hear they're expecting some intense fighting. We should be getting reports any day now. Do you have anyone special in that camp?"

"A good friend," Emily said. "A really good friend. There are also lots of people we know socially, even if they aren't really close. But some of the women in this camp have husbands over there. We're all very worried. We'd like to know if they're all right."

He smiled. "Sure thing. As soon as I hear anything, I'll let you girls know. How about I meet you at the front gate-or what's left of the front gate-tomorrow at noon? I think we should get a report by then."

They agreed, and began their walk back to the camp, their shopping bags filled with food to bring back to camp. They were being careful not to overeat, but the chow line at camp was still pretty meager, in spite of the addition of food contributed by the army, as well as Red Cross packages. As they passed a stall that sold ribbons, Jeannie grabbed Emily's arm.

"Look! Ribbons! I want to get one for my hair. Do we have any money left?"

"Not much, but I think it'll be enough for a ribbon. We're running low, but I heard we would be able to draw on the Army for emergency funds in a couple of days. Let's get you a ribbon."

They found a nice satin ribbon in Jeannie's favorite shade of blue, one that just matched her eyes. Jeannie was ecstatic. It was the first new, pretty thing she had owned in three and a half years.

"What about you, Emily? Don't you want anything?"

"No, I don't think so. Oh, wait-I see some nice combs. Maybe a couple of tortoise shell combs for my hair."

They stopped at the stall and bargained with the vendor for a while. Emily got two little combs at nearly a prewar price, and tried not to feel a twinge of guilt at the thought of spending the money. She picked up one larger comb for her mother and barrettes for Charlie and Annabelle.

Now, the whole family had new hair ornaments! As she surveyed her purchases, she decided it was worth it. They could survive until the stipends from the Army came in, and their morale could use the boost of something pretty. She put the twin combs in her hair, making graceful wings on each side of her face.

"Too bad we don't have any rats for our hair," said Jeannie.

"We spent them," giggled Emily, remembering the hair "rats" made of rolls of money they'd brought into camp.

When they returned to camp, they told Margarete about their meeting with the tall sergeant. Much to Emily's surprise, her mother made no objection to them speaking with a stranger. "After all, girls," she said, "He is one of the men who rescued us. Surely that needs no formal introduction."

She was also pleased with their purchases, and called the younger girls immediately so they could put their new barrettes in their hair. They were delighted, and Margarete herself expressed her appreciation for the large comb, which she used to secure her hair in a twist at the back of her head.

"It feels so nice to be well groomed," she murmured. She had been working on mending their clothing. She drew a few folded bills out of an inner pocket of one of her dresses.

"Here, Emily," she said. "Tomorrow, why don't you and Jeannie go and buy some fabric, and a spool of thread? I might be able to make blouses for you all. See if you can get six yards."

The girls agreed, and said they would go out at noon. They told her they were meeting Sgt. Francis at the gate, and Margarete was pleased they would have an escort.

"It's so dangerous now," she said, "with all those nasty bombs falling. He sounds like a nice young man. I think you'll be safer with him than walking around Manila on your own."

The next morning, the two sisters got up and dressed cheerfully, in better spirits than they had been in years. The new ribbons and combs were put to good use, and they chattered brightly through breakfast, as if they didn't have a care in the world.

Breakfast was a nice surprise--pancakes, real American pancakes, with syrup. The Army cook supervising the meal explained that there were extra eggs in the batter, but they didn't dare give the prisoners even a whole egg each. Doctor's orders. They were afraid of something called protein poisoning, which was a risk when someone who has been deprived of protein for a long time is able to eat normal amounts. The cook explained he was under orders to increase their protein amounts gradually. They hoped the prisoners would be able to travel in a month or two, and by then, as he put it, "we'll have whupped the enemy's rear end all the way back to Japan and you can take a ship back to the good old U. S. of A. in perfect safety."

Of course, there was the little matter of the war. Fighting was still going on in the Philippines. Bob brought them interesting news; he was staying in Manila to continue the fighting, but a large air strike was planned for Los Baños. He couldn't tell them the details, but assured them their friends stood a good chance of being rescued in time.

The days passed, and Emily and her family grew stronger. Margarete was distressed that she had as yet received no news of her husband. She held out some hope that he might be in Los Baños. However, when the long-awaited liberation of that camp happened some three weeks after the liberation of Santo Tomas, his name was not on a list of the prisoners. To Emily's delight, James Harper was listed as among the rescued, in a state of near-starvation but alive. The prisoners were receiving much-needed medical care and they would be brought to Manila as soon as the fighting in the capital was over.

In early March, an official dispatch brought the bad news to Margarete. Her husband's death was confirmed. Heartbroken, she seemed to dwindle over night from a strong, assertive matriarch to a frail old woman who was completely incapable of making decisions. Much to her dismay, the entire task of leadership in the family fell on Emily. She was the one who carefully rationed their money to secure clothes for her sisters and mother, get medical care for their numerous ills, and finally, book passage to the States on a military ship.

Partly because of Bob Francis' insistence that California was the only place to be, Jeannie persuaded Emily to take a ship heading for Los Angeles. The repatriation money from the U. S. government would help them get set up when they got there, but she and Emily would have to get jobs as soon as they arrived.

"You can get a good job as a secretary, Emily," said Jeannie. "I don't know what I could do. My only job here was as a nursing assistant, and I don't know if they would think I'm qualified."

"Sure they will. You'll find a job right away. We both will! From what I hear, women are getting into all kinds of jobs back in the States. There'll be no problem at all." Emily wasn't as sure as she sounded, but she was determined to maintain a positive outlook. Jeannie was guardedly optimistic, but she had her moments of depression.

Charlie was still determined to join the military in one of the women's services, either the Women's Army Corps or the Navy equivalent, the WAVES. At seventeen, she was old enough if her mother gave her consent. Unfortunately, Margarete was in no shape to make any kind of decision. When Charlie asked her about it, she burst into tears.

Emily was deeply shaken at the depth of her mother's grief. Sometimes, she found herself resenting it. She had known about her father's death for years, and for her mother's sake had kept the information to herself. She hadn't broken down, but had gone on doing what needed to be done. Now, when her mother knew the worst, she expected her mother to be as strong as she had always been. Margarete had never fallen apart like this before. She had been the family's rock, its tower of strength. Now, she couldn't even decide what dress to wear, and some days just stayed in bed.

Emily felt the burden of caring for her family was crushing, but did her best not to let it show. After all, her last words from her father had been to take care of the family. Had he known? Not that he was going to die, of course, but that if he did, had he known that Margarete would collapse. The more she thought about it, the more Emily thought it was so. Her father had known his wife very well and certainly could read her character. He probably knew Margarete had been pushed to the limit of her endurance, and without him, she would lose her own prop, her own tower of strength. She would be unable to lend strength to anyone else. Realizing this, he had handed the charge over to Emily. She was determined not to let him down.

With Jeannie's help, Emily organized the family's move to the United States. Their property in the Philippines was destroyed. The Japanese had burned the house, and although the fields were still there, and the trees that yielded fiber for rope and produced coconuts, without the house it would be a difficult proposition for five women alone to make a go of it and rebuild. They turned the property over to a distant cousin, who had a large family and was willing to work hard to build up the plantation again. Their lives were going to undergo monumental changes. None of them had ever been to the States. Her father had, but none of the rest of them had. Her mother had been born in British North Borneo, and the rest of them were born in the Philippines. They had lived on the islands all their lives. How would they adjust to life in what was truly almost a foreign country to them?

They were limited in the amount of baggage they could take. However, they were used to living on nothing, and being able to bring two suitcases each was a luxury. They had part of their repatriation money and they were promised the rest when they reached Los Angeles. Each of them had several changes of clothing and all the necessary accessories, as well as toilet articles and cosmetics. They were still skinny, but no longer looked half-starved. Fashionably slim, Emily preferred to think of it.

The day of departure, they arrived with their baggage at the dock. Emily scanned the passenger manifest, and was pleased to see the Harper family was listed—all but Kells, who she had heard was remaining in the Philippines with his wife to help run her family's business. Emily wondered if she would get a chance to talk with James on shipboard. She hoped so. They had so much to talk about!

She wanted to hear all about the rescue of the prisoners in his camp. That information hadn't been circulated to the general public as yet. Even Bob had been unwilling to share the news, as it was classified. However, James would be able to tell her, since he wasn't military. She was also looking forward to talking to him about the situation with her mother's depression and the family's situation. He might have some useful advice. Over the years in which she had been writing to him, she had gained an appreciation for his understanding and wisdom.

She and her sisters and mother got on the ship and settled in to their bunks in the quarters below. There were large rooms with stacks of bunks, seven high, packed so closely together that it was impossible to sit up on a bunk. It was cramped and uncomfortable, but the price was right. The family couldn't afford regular passenger accommodations, even if normal shipping lines had been running during wartime. This was a military transport, and the facilities reminded Emily of the description of crew's quarters in seafaring novels like *Mutiny on the Bounty* and *Two Years Before the Mast*. It was a good thing she wasn't claustrophobic! Anything but—in fact, the last three years of fear had developed in Emily a fondness for small hiding places. Still, this was positively tiny.

"Talk about being crammed in like sardines," exclaimed Charlie. "We'll need a can opener to move around down here."

She had a point. There was barely room to stow all their belongings in the cargo hold, and only a small bag of personal items could be taken into the sleeping area. It didn't take long to unpack. Once that was accomplished, they went up on deck to watch the departure and wave good-bye to the Philippines—perhaps forever.

Chapter Thirteen

The first night at sea, Emily couldn't sleep. There had been so much stress involved with getting the family ready to move, getting them settled on shipboard, and worrying about the future that she just couldn't settle down in her cramped, stuffy bunk. Normally, she didn't mind closed-in spaces, but right now, she found it oppressive. Besides, Jeannie snored, however much she might deny it as "unladylike." Emily dressed silently, so as not to awaken the others, and went up on deck.

The moon was beautiful, a silvery crescent gleaming down on the rippling waters of the Pacific. Emily leaned against the rail, letting the welcome cool breezes ruffle her hair. This was much better than the bunkroom! Just knowing they were safe and on their way to the United States, to that almost mythical land of her ancestors, was the best part. Here she was, on an American ship. The war was over. All the fighting and turmoil was at an end. She felt an unfamiliar stirring; was it hope?

Perhaps. She had scarcely dared hope for anything beyond mere survival for so long it was hard to recognize the feeling.

Suddenly the peace of the evening was shattered by loud, rowdy voices. Three sailors, no doubt off duty, came strolling down the deck, laughing uproariously. Emily shrank against the rail, trying to look inconspicuous, but without success.

"Hey, lookit here! Who's this?" called out one of them, a big burly fellow with red hair.

"Wow, she's a looker. Where you been all my life, cute thing?" chimed in another sailor, a short, wiry lad with freckles.

"Outa my way, guys, I saw her first," said a slim, dark-haired sailor with a moustache and a tattoo on his arm.

They came up to Emily, grinning and laughing. She looked away, trying to show them by her rigid back and firm posture that she was not interested in conversation.

"Hey, come on, pretty thing, talk to a lonely sailor," said the redhead.

Emily turned to them. "I don't think it's a good idea, boys. I'm engaged to be married, and he's very jealous. You'd better move on."

"Engaged? Well, so what? He ain't here, is he?" the redhead replied.

Emily thought frantically. Technically, what she said was true; she was still engaged, but her real fiancé was somewhere in the wide world, if he was still alive, and she had no idea how to reach him. If she told them the truth about his whereabouts, the sailors would continue to bother her, probably for the entire voyage. On the other hand, she couldn't very well claim her fiancé was on the ship. They'd want to know his name, and would probably check the roster to see if she was telling the truth. What could she do? There was no question of being friendly with the sailors. They were rough, and a bit frightening. She could smell liquor on their breath. They also smelled like they hadn't bathed recently. She was starting to get dizzy, and was afraid she might faint. How strange, that she'd stood up to their Japanese captors and was afraid of American sailors! She'd been brave enough during the war, especially with the radio, and the letters she wrote to Jimmy to get information to the other prison camp …

That was it! "Yes, he is here," she said. "He's on this ship."

"Oh, yeah? What's his name?" the little one asked.

"James Harper. He's another ex-POW," she said. "He survived some pretty nasty things in camp. I don't think he'll take too kindly to you trying to move in on his territory, and there's not much that scares him anymore. Not after the things he's been through."

Suddenly the sailors' attitude changed. They had a great deal of respect for the people who had survived being imprisoned by the enemy for so long. Even experienced sailors and soldiers knew the prisoners had often suffered things they could only imagine.

"Sorry, ma'am," the dark sailor said. "We didn't know. Didn't mean to give any offense, you know. Just being friendly."

"That's right," said the redhead. "You tell this Harper guy we were as polite as can be. Not that the Navy's afraid of anyone, no sir, but we don't want to show any disrespect to any of our men."

Emily nodded, and the sailors moved on.

She was alone on the deck once more, and faced with a dilemma. What to do next? She had to get in touch with Jimmy right away. The sailors might check out her story, and it would be embarrassing if they went to apologize to him and he had no idea what they were talking about.

She went back down to the living quarters. The names of people in each room were printed on a card taped outside the door. It seemed she had read a hundred cards before she found the Harper family's room. Tentatively, she knocked on the door, half-hoping there would be no answer.

The door opened to reveal Beth Harper's familiar face, her hair done up in curling rags. "Emily! Fancy meeting you here! We do run into each other in the strangest places."

"Beth, is Jimmy here? I need to talk to him for just a moment."

Beth raised her plucked eyebrows. "Certainly. I'll call him." But that wasn't necessary; he was right at her shoulder, and stepped quickly out of the room with a smile for his sister and an even bigger smile for Emily.

"Querida!" he said cheerfully, using the Spanish word for "darling." Emily blushed. She hadn't realized how awkward it would seem, asking him to pretend they were engaged when they had just spent the last two years writing romantic letters to one another in Spanish. "What can I do for you?"

She looked up into his brown eyes. She remembered that he normally wore glasses; she assumed they'd been lost in camp and he hadn't replaced them. He wasn't bad looking, either. Not a movie star type, of course, but a nice looking guy. He was about six feet tall and very thin—all of them were thin, with brown hair and eyes that crinkled when he smiled. He was smiling right now.

"Actually, this is a bit embarrassing," she admitted. She told him about the incident with the sailors, and his smile just kept getting bigger.

"It's not funny," she said, and he shook his head.

"I'm not laughing," he said. "I think it's great. This should be a lot of fun. We'll need to take long walks on the deck, of course, just to keep up the pretense. We might as well start right away. Are you ready?" He offered his arm, and she took it, wondering what she had gotten herself into.

Chapter Fourteen

The trip to California took two weeks. During that time, Emily went on many long walks with James. They strolled on the deck, went to dinner together in the dining room—Emily was never sure whether to call it a galley or a mess hall—and watched fourteen sunsets over the Pacific from the stern of the ship.

James insisted on acting as if they were really engaged. "After all," he said, "I wouldn't want those sailors to find out what a little fibber you are. I'm just thinking of your reputation."

"Sure you are," said Emily. Sometimes his sense of humor got on her nerves.

"Besides, who knows? You might decide I'm not such a bad bargain. Maybe we should really be engaged."

"Not on your life! I wouldn't marry you if you were the last man on earth," insisted Emily. "You're just not my type."

"Wanna bet?"

"What are you talking about?"

Jimmy grinned. "I said, wanna bet? I'll give you ten-to-one odds."

"What does that mean? I'm not a gambler, you know," Emily said, as if she hadn't spent a few afternoons at the races before the war.

"Simple. We'll bet a dollar. At ten to one, that's ten dollars plus your original dollar. If you never marry me, I'll owe you eleven dollars. Now, isn't that a deal?"

"That's outrageous. I wouldn't bet on something like that."

"Why not?" he asked, still grinning. "Afraid you'll lose?"

"Of course not. Since you put it that way, I'll take your bet."

"It's a deal. Ten to one. I'll make it easier. The bet is that you'll marry me before the year is out."

"No fear of that. This will be the easiest money I've ever earned!" Emily smiled sweetly. Right then, she decided that on New Year's Eve she'd contact him, wherever he was, and demand her eleven dollars. That would show him she wasn't a silly girl to joke around with. They continued their walk around the deck of the ship, with Emily in a more cheerful mood than she had been in many days.

"What do you want to do after the war?" Emily asked Jimmy on one of their walks. They were due to arrive in Los Angeles the next day, and she felt a little bit sad that the voyage was about to end.

"Well, my degree is in civil engineering. I figure there'll be lots of government jobs opening up. I hear the U. S. Government will be doing some pretty heavy rebuilding in countries affected by the war. I figure there will be job openings for engineers to work on those projects, like building hospitals, airports, and so on. Who knows? If they do a lot of work in Manila, I might even wind up back there."

"Would you want to?"

"Sure. I know the people and the languages. I wouldn't mind seeing the rest of the world, though. I haven't seen Europe yet, and I've always wondered about Africa. Would you like to travel?

"I don't know. I think I'll be busy getting my family settled in California. It's all on my shoulders now, you know." Emily sighed.

Sometimes it seemed the burden was a little bit too heavy.

"Well, they look sturdy enough for the job," he observed, grinning.

"That shows what you know about women," Emily retorted. "Women don't want to be broad-shouldered and sturdy. We want to be fragile and cherished."

"You've got to be kidding," Jimmy said. "There's nothing fragile about you. A fragile, helpless clinging type? Not you. Your sister, maybe, but not you."

"That's another thing that's always bothered me. Whenever we double dated, the men always asked Jeannie if she was too cold and wanted the car window closed or too hot and wanted it open. No one ever asked me if I was comfortable. "

Jimmy stopped and looked closely at her. "You're serious, aren't you? You aren't kidding. Hey, kid, don't you know that men don't really want women to be helpless? Not real women, anyway. They want women to be … well, just people, sort of like short men, only lots prettier. That's the difference between girls and women. Girls are fragile.

Women aren't. Not women of character, anyway, and that's what you are. A woman of character. A take-charge kind of gal. Don't you know that?"

"I guess so, but I don't want to be. Just once, I want to be the one that's taken care of, not the one who's taking care of everyone else. Is that too much to ask?"

He looked down at her, his brown eyes full of meaning.

"No, it isn't," he said softly. "Not too much at all."

They continued walking around the deck, hand in hand, as the moon came out from behind the clouds and wove a bright highway on the water, pointing the way to a new life in California.

Epilogue

They got married, of course. They reached California. Jimmy got a job with the United States War Damage Commission and he was sent back to Manila to oversee the rebuilding of the Philippines in the post-war years. Then, he went on to a career in the Foreign Service, where Emily was one of the most delightful diplomatic wives ever to grace a formal reception. He made a promise to Emily on their wedding day. He promised he would always take care of her and her family. He kept that promise.

He also kept his sense of humor. The moment they were married, as they were walking out of the church building, he said, in his most tender voice:

"OK, kid, where's my eleven dollars?"

About the Author

Therese "Terry" Martin is the daughter of John and Evelyn Hackett, career Foreign Service personnel with the U. S. State Department. She grew up in various places around the world, from Hue, the ancient imperial capital of Vietnam, to Monrovia, Liberia, West Africa, with time out to attend schools in the Philippines, Spain, and Italy. An avid reader from the age of three, she began writing fiction when she was seven years old. Her first sales were made under duress to guests at her parents' dinner parties. Unfortunately, she spent the pennies gained from these efforts on candy, and decided there was no more money to be made in the publishing business. Nevertheless, she continued to write, and has published over 200 nonfiction articles and four volumes of a K-12 social studies-based unit study curriculum for home schools.

After some years in the world of business—insurance, real estate, and lending—and a brief fling in politics, she found her true calling in education, and enjoys teaching history, Latin, and literature to middle school students. Her undergraduate degree is in liberal arts, and she holds a master's degree in education from Regis University. She lives in Castle Rock, Colorado, within sight of Pike's Peak. She is married, with four sons, two granddaughters, and four grandchildren of the heart.